The Best Of
The Mailbox®

Learning Centers
Intermediate

Editor In Chief:
Marge Michel

Product Director:
Kathy Wolf

Editors:
Becky Andrews, Carol Rawleigh

Artists:
Pam Crane
Sheila Krill
Rob Mayworth
Barry Slate

Cover Design:
Jim Counts

About This Book

The Best Of *The Mailbox*® Learning Centers Intermediate is a collection of the best learning centers published in the Intermediate editions of *The Mailbox*® magazine from 1988 to 1994. It is designed to provide an extensive collection of skill-specific, teacher-created, easy-to-make learning centers for today's busy teacher. The learning centers include an illustration, complete instructions, and corresponding reproducible patterns.

Table Of Contents

Language Arts

Vocabulary 4–6

Grammar 7–10

Reading 11–14

Research Skills 15–17

Writing 18–31

Math 19–42

Thinking Skills 43

Geography 44–45

Multi-Skill Centers 46–49

Seasonal & Holiday 50–56

Miscellaneous Tips & Ideas 57–61

Patterns 62–112

Hang In There!

Add a little zest to weekly vocabulary exercises with the reproducible activity center on page 62. Duplicate page 62; then have a student color the page with colorful markers. Glue the page to a sheet of construction paper and laminate it. Use a wipe-off marker to label the center with the week's vocabulary or spelling words. Post the sheet on a bulletin board or at a center for students to work on during free time. Wipe the sheet clean at the end of the week, and it is ready for a new list of words on Monday.

The Word Garden

Vocabulary will grow in this garden as children match prefix flowers to word roots. Duplicate the pattern on page 63; then glue it inside a file folder. After coloring the flowers inside, laminate the folder; then program the flowers as shown with a wipe-off marker. Reprogram the folder frequently with new prefixes or suffixes. Give a "green thumb" award to students who create the most new words.

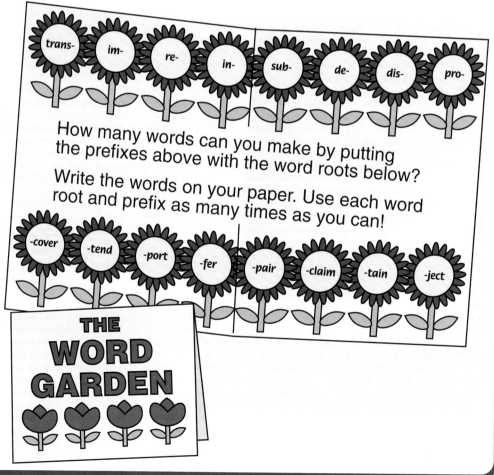

Adjective And Noun Ding-a-lings

Use riddles to encourage vocabulary development. After explaining the use of a thesaurus, have each child think of a noun and an adjective that rhyme. Using synonyms, each child creates a clue to the rhyming words. On the front of a cut-out bell (see the patterns on page 64) each student writes his clue. Turning the bell over and upside down, he writes the answer. After checking their riddles with the teacher, students staple the bells to a bulletin board. Children will want to create additional ding-a-lings, using more and more obscure vocabulary to stump their friends.

Jane M. Miller
Muncie Elementary School
Leavenworth, KS

New-To-Me Words

Combine vocabulary studies with reading, dictionary skills, and penmanship—all in one center! Place current magazines and newspapers, scissors, tape, and dictionaries at a center. Duplicate and color the pattern on page 65; then mount it on a piece of tagboard, adding the title and directions as shown. Display the poster at the center. Each week challenge every student to find a word that is unfamiliar to him in a newspaper or magazine article, then follow the steps on the poster.

Mark Peterson—Gr. 6
Montrose, SD

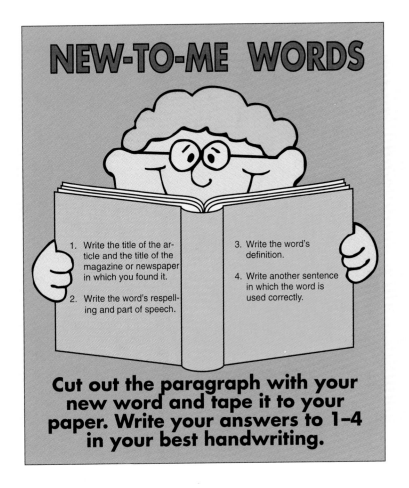

NEW-TO-ME WORDS

1. Write the title of the article and the title of the magazine or newspaper in which you found it.

2. Write the word's respelling and part of speech.

3. Write the word's definition.

4. Write another sentence in which the word is used correctly.

Cut out the paragraph with your new word and tape it to your paper. Write your answers to 1–4 in your best handwriting.

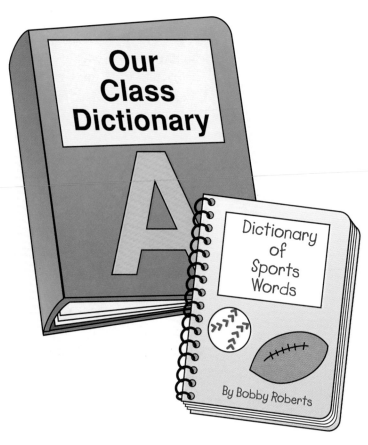

Build A Dictionary

Celebrate Noah Webster's finest accomplishment by setting up a center for young lexicographers! At a center, display a collection of several different types of dictionaries. (Ask your librarian for help.) Purchase 26 small, inexpensive notebooks. Label the front of each with a letter of the alphabet; then store the notebooks in a decorated box or basket. Whenever a student finds an interesting new word, have him write it and its definition in the appropriate notebook. Encourage students to write their own dictionaries on topics of interest such as cooking, sports, or "Big Words To Impress Other Kids And Adults."

Catch Feline Fever

Here's a "purr-fectly" clever way to practice dictionary skills. Duplicate and cut out the worksheet on page 66. Glue it inside the folder as shown. Cut out and color the cat pattern on page 66; then glue it to the front of the folder as shown. Provide an answer key for self-checking.

Michelle Martin
Macon, GA

Key
1. catapult
2. caterpillar
3. catalpa
4. catalog
5. cattle
6. catsup
7. cataract
8. catcher
9. catnip
10. catastrophe
11. cattails
12. catacomb
13. cataclysm
14. category

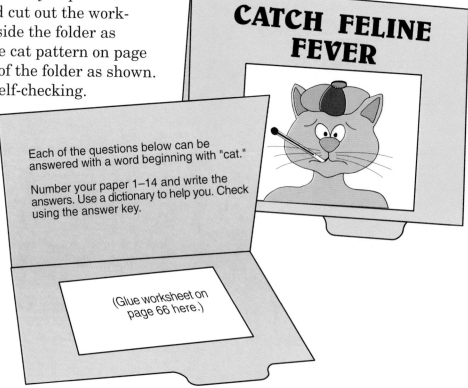

CATCH FELINE FEVER

Each of the questions below can be answered with a word beginning with "cat."

Number your paper 1–14 and write the answers. Use a dictionary to help you. Check using the answer key.

(Glue worksheet on page 66 here.)

Who Did It?

Challenge students to solve a kidnapping mystery while practicing grammar skills. Duplicate page 67. After a student colors the suspect pictures for you, glue them as shown on the left side of a folder. Staple the sentences also on page 67 on the right side of the folder as shown. Place an answer key in a pocket attached to the back of the folder. Staple a new set of sentences inside the folder each week, making a different suspect the guilty party. (Since the numbers of the incorrect sentences add up to 58, Suzanne the maid is the guilty party this time.)

Student directions:
You are a detective investigating the kidnapping of Marvin Moneybags. The six suspects are pictured here.

Read the sentences for clues about the suspects. On your own paper, correct any sentences with grammatical errors. Add up the numbers of the incorrect sentences to discover the kidnapper's identity. Check the key.

Who Did It?

1. "Jane and me went shopping that morning," said Mona.
2. Jane and Mona is in real trouble.
3. Jane gave the candlestick to her father as a gift.
4. Sidney likes to play tennis.
5. Does Jane and Sidney play tennis together?
6. Sam found a tennis racket beside the ransom note.
7. A pillow lay on the floor beside Marvin's bed.
8. A book lied open on the table.
9. Suzanne said, "Hand me one of them books."
10. "Sit the book on the table there," said Sam.
11. Suzanne has really growed up.
12. Jake didn't never like Marvin.

Comic Strip Contractions

Looking for a fun way to review contractions? The comic strips are full of them! Cut out several cartoons with examples of contractions in the captions. Circle the contractions and mount the strips inside a file folder. Write student directions inside the folder. Laminate the folder for durability. Place the file folder and the funny papers at a center.

Kathy M. Peterson
Alpha, IL

Student Directions:
Find 10 contractions in the comic strips. Cut out and glue the comic strip pictures to a sheet of paper. Circle the contractions; then write the two words that make each contraction.

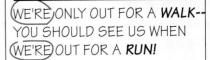

WE'RE ONLY OUT FOR A **WALK**-- YOU SHOULD SEE US WHEN WE'RE OUT FOR A **RUN!**

Spelling Demons

Use this center year-round for practicing "tricky" words that students often misspell. Have students make these "spelling demons" by decorating small lidded boxes with construction paper, felt, and other art materials. Inside each box, glue a list of five to ten misspelled spelling demons (see the list below). Glue an answer key to the bottom of the box. The student takes a demon to his desk, opens it to read the incorrect words, then spells them correctly on his paper. He turns the demon over to check his work.

about	cousin	often	terrible
absence	dairy	piece	though
accept	didn't	poison	thought
advise	enough	principal	through
all right	favorite	principle	tomorrow
although	February	quit	trouble
among	fierce	quite	Tuesday
aunt	friend	receive	vacation
awhile	guard	rough	weigh
because	handkerchief	several	were
believe	height	skiing	where
bought	instead	straight	which
built	knew	surprise	writing
chocolate	know	surround	your
cough	neither	tear	you're

Laurie Vent
Upper Sandusky, OH

Puzzle Match

Here's an idea for recycling old coffee cans or whipped cream lids. Label each of four lids with a part of speech: noun, verb, adjective, adverb. Trace and cut out four construction-paper circles the same size as the lids. Cut each circle into sections. Be sure that each circle is cut differently to make the activity self-checking. On the sections of one circle, write words that are nouns. On the sections of the other circles, write verbs, adjectives, and adverbs. Students reassemble the circles by placing each section in the correct lid.

Sharleen Berg—Gr. 3–4
St. Peter's School
Jefferson, SD

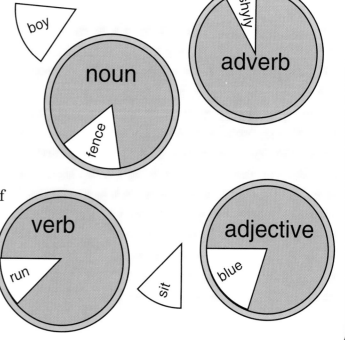

Word Web

Students won't mind getting caught up in this web to practice parts of speech. Inside a file folder, glue two copies of the web gameboard on page 68. Label each spider's body with a part of speech; then have a student color the spider bodies. Write the numbered sentences below on paper circles that fit inside milk jug lids. In each sentence, underline one word. Provide an answer key that tells the parts of speech of the underlined words. Glue a simple spider picture inside each of four other lids.

Each child, in turn, chooses a lid, identifies the part of speech, and covers that spider on his gameboard. If a spider picture is drawn, the player can use it to cover any spider on his gameboard. The first player to cover all of his spiders wins!

Jean O. Youngsteadt
Springfield, MO

Student Directions:

1. Place the lids facedown. Each player chooses a web gameboard.
2. In turn, draw a lid. Say the part of speech of the underlined word; then have your partner check the key.
3. If correct, place the lid on that spider on your gameboard. If incorrect, or if that space is already covered, your turn is over.
4. If you draw a spider lid, you may use it to cover any space on your gameboard.
5. The first player to cover all of his spiders wins!

Sentences:

1. <u>Most</u> spiders make silken egg cases. *(adjective)*
2. The spider caught the fly and wrapped <u>it</u> in silk. *(pronoun)*
3. When a male jumping spider finds a mate, <u>he</u> dances. *(pronoun)*
4. The female spider <u>guards</u> the egg sac. *(verb)*
5. Jumping spiders <u>leap</u> on their prey. *(verb)*
6. Spiders have no <u>wings</u>. *(noun)*
7. Some spiders live in trees <u>and</u> bushes. *(conjunction)*
8. <u>Oh</u>, there's a brown recluse spider! *(interjection)*
9. Some spiders live <u>in</u> the grass. *(preposition)*
10. A spider bites <u>quickly</u> when it captures its prey. *(adverb)*
11. Wolf spiders see <u>well</u>. *(adverb)*
12. The black widow spider is <u>poisonous</u>. *(adjective)*
13. Brown recluse spiders are sometimes found in old <u>attics</u>. *(noun)*
14. The black widow has a red hourglass shape <u>on</u> its back. *(preposition)*
15. <u>Wow</u>! That tarantula is huge! *(interjection)*
16. Tarantulas look mean, <u>but</u> only hurt or frightened spiders will bite. *(conjunction)*

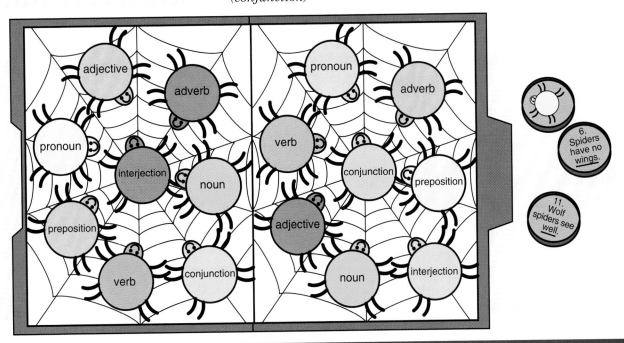

Welcome Back To The Future!

For this verb tense learning center, ask students to illustrate characters from the past, present, and future. Post these pictures on a bulletin board near a center. Duplicate page 69; then glue the page on tagboard, cut out the wheels, and place them at the center.

Have students work at this center in pairs. In turn, have each partner use a pencil point and paper clip as shown to spin the verb wheel. After he writes the word on his paper, have the student spin the tense wheel and write the correct form of the verb. Once each student has spun each wheel five times, have the pair use the verbs in a collaborative story that involves one or more of the characters on the bulletin board.

Jewel Harmon
Johnson County Middle School
Mountain City, TN

All Boxed Up

Turn small empty tissue boxes into handy sorting centers for parts-of-speech practice. Attach a pocket labeled with a different part of speech to each side of the box. Label a supply of tagboard strips with numbered sentences in which you've underlined one word. Store the strips in the center of the box. Students pull out the strips and place each one in the correct pocket. Provide an answer key for student checking.

Susan Nixon
Avondale, AZ

1. He <u>ran</u> in the race.

2. The <u>shoelace</u> is broken.

NOUN   VERB

Choose five idioms.
Draw a picture to
illustrate each idiom.

1. Lend me your ear.
2. Don't run off at the mouth.
3. I've got my eye on you.
4. She has a sharp tongue.
5. Better shake a leg.
6. I gave him a tongue-lashing.

7. He has a nose for news.
8. She's all ears.
9. He's a heel.
10. Lend me a hand.
11. She's a real busybody.
12. Get off my back!

Shake a leg?

"Idiomagic!"

No bones about it, your students will be all ears when you introduce this comical idiom center. Duplicate the pattern on page 70. Then color the pattern, cut it out, and glue it inside a folder as shown. List the twelve idioms in the folder. Direct students to illustrate five of the idioms listed. Label and display the drawings for a center sure to tickle your funny bone!

Book Mobiles

The elements of a favorite book are brought into focus with this center activity. Post a list of story elements at the center. Provide construction paper strips, yarn, a hole punch, scissors, and coat hangers. Students write each story element on a strip; then, using their books, they write a description of each element on the back. Completed strips are hung with a yarn from coat hangers as shown. Invite students to share completed mobiles before displaying the projects in the classroom.

Sr. Ann Claire Rhoads
Mother Seton School
Emmitsburg, MD

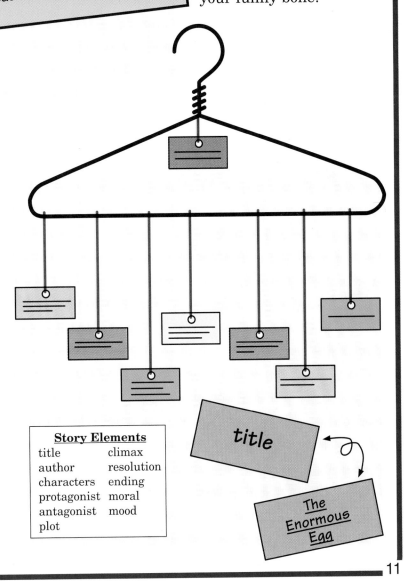

Story Elements	
title	climax
author	resolution
characters	ending
protagonist	moral
antagonist	mood
plot	

title

The Enormous Egg

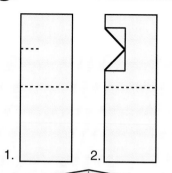

Pop-Up Cards

Reading a set of directions and then following them is a skill students often struggle with. Give your kids some practice that's also poppin' good fun with this idea. Provide paper, scissors, and directions at a center. Have children follow the instructions to make these unique, pop-up cards.

1. Fold a piece of paper in half lengthwise.
2. Lightly draw a 1 1/2-inch horizontal line in the middle of the top half. (Figure 1.)
3. Cut through the fold along this line.
4. Fold both sides of the cut line back. (Figure 2.)
5. Open the paper with the cutout at the top of the page.
6. Fold top to bottom.
7. Fold again left to right so the cutout is inside the book.
8. Lift the top and bottom part of the cutout so it moves when you open and close the card.
9. Create a picture using the cutout. (Figure 3.)

Sandra L. Howe
Honolulu, HI

Target Practice

Take aim at syllabication rules! Label target cutouts (patterns on page 71) with two-syllable words. Laminate several tagboard arrows (pattern on page 71), then cut them out. Store the arrows and targets in press-on pockets attached to the inside of the folder. Provide a wipe-off marker. For self-checking, write the correct word division on the back of each target.

Cathie Weaver
Wesley Christian School
Springfield, GA

Target words:

totem	robin
paper	linen
spider	pony
solid	river
never	cabin

Write each target word on an arrow, dividing it into syllables. Turn the target over to check.

RULES
1. When there is a consonant between the two vowels, and the first vowel is short, divide <u>after</u> the consonant.

2. When there is a consonant between two vowels, and the first vowel is long, divide <u>before</u> the consonant.

Toying With Cause And Effect

Simple toddler toys are the only items needed in this clever language arts center. I gather several toys that represent cause-and-effect relationships, such as a pull toy that makes noise and a jack-in-the-box. I then number each toy as a station. As pairs of students visit each station, they observe and play with the toys. Students then describe each toy in a cause-and-effect sentence. After visiting (and playing!) in each station, we gather together to share our sentences and observations.

Jane E. Minnick—Gr. 5
McEowen Elementary
Harrisonville, MO

Sock Puppets

Here's an art activity that's perfect for providing practice in following directions. Place all of the materials along with the illustrated directions at a center, and let students create sock puppets. Later, children can name their characters and write and produce a puppet show.

Dr. Sam Ed Brown
College of Education
Texas Woman's University
Denton, TX

Materials: one sock, fabric scissors, red cloth, red thread, two or three matching buttons, needle, embroidery needle and thread, yarn

Student Directions:
1. Cut through the double thickness of the foot of the sock as shown.
2. Cut a piece of red cloth. Make it as wide as the sock and twice as long as the cut portion of the sock. This will become the mouth of the puppet.
3. Turn the sock inside out. Sew the mouth to the sock with red thread.
4. Turn the sock right side out, and attach buttons for eyes.
5. Embroider a nose on the sock or use a button.
6. Sew on yarn hair.
7. Name your puppet! Get together with a friend, and write a script for a puppet show.

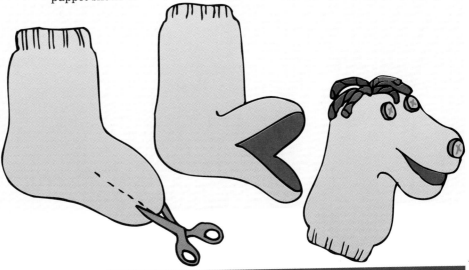

Fishy Facts

There's nothing fishy about the facts and opinions practice this center activity offers! Label the outside of a folder with the title "Fishy Facts" and pictures of aquarium-related items. Duplicate two copies of the aquarium pattern on page 72. After coloring the aquariums, glue them inside the folder as shown. Write the following facts and opinions on fish cutouts (patterns on page 81.) Label each fish FACT or OPINION on the back for self-checking. Have students place each statement on its appropriate aquarium.

FACTS
- An aquarist is a person who has an aquarium.
- For most tropical fish the water should be kept between 72° and 80°F.
- Young fish are called fry.
- Fish should be given only the amount of food that they can eat in about five minutes.
- The filter helps keep the water clean.
- Plants help produce oxygen for the fish to breathe.
- Very large tanks for saltwater animals are oceanariums.

OPINIONS
- Tropical fish are beautiful.
- It's fun to set up an aquarium.
- Colorful gravel is better for aquariums.
- Every aquarium should have a snail.
- Saltwater aquariums are better than freshwater aquariums.
- The sea horse is the most interesting fish.
- Fish are great pets.

Cathie Weaver
Springfield Elementary
Springfield, GA

Bananas About Books!

In this learning center, your students will find a tasty bunch of writing activities to complete as they independently read novels, basal stories, or other materials. Duplicate the activity cards on pages 74–77. Mount them on construction paper. Laminate the cards and cut them apart. Display the cards at a center entitled "We're Bananas About Books!" Duplicate a copy of the contract on page 73 for each child. Have students attach their contracts to folders which they've decorated. As students complete the tasks, they place them in the folders and color the corresponding bananas on their contracts.

What does IBM stand for?

Where is Angel Falls?

Where is the Wailing Wall?

The Olde Curiosity Shoppe

Shopping for a nifty research skills center? Duplicate the pattern on page 78; then have a student volunteer color it and glue it to the lid of a gift box or the front of an empty cereal box. Fill the box with numbered trivia questions, each written on a small square of brightly colored paper which has been folded to conceal the question. When a student has free time, let her choose a question from the box and research its answer in an encyclopedia. Besides learning how to find information quickly, your students will begin to leaf through encyclopedias and rush to your desk to share an interesting new topic or fact.

Karoleigh K. Nitchman—Grs. 4–6
Hurtsboro School Foundation
Hurtsboro, AL

United Nations Station

Celebrate the diverse countries of our world while reviewing how to write a good report. Duplicate the United Nations emblem on page 79; then glue it to a piece of poster board labeled with the directions shown. Place the poster, the list of countries below, and reference books in a special area of your room. Provide time for students to share their reports. Post the flags on a bulletin board.

List of countries:

Argentina	Ethiopia	Italy	Poland
Australia	France	Japan	Portugal
Belgium	Greece	Libya	South Africa
Canada	Guatemala	Netherlands	Spain
Chile	Hungary	New Zealand	Sweden
Congo	India	Norway	Thailand
Denmark	Ireland	Pakistan	Turkey
Egypt	Israel	Panama	Venezuela

United Nations Station

1. Select a country that appeals to you from the list. Write your initials beside the country.
2. Use reference books to take notes on your country. Follow this outline:
   I.   Geography
   II. Most important products
   III. Ethnic groups
   IV. Interesting customs
   V.   Kinds of agriculture and business
   VI. Political system
3. Use your notes to write one paragraph on each topic in the outline.
4. After proofreading your report, rewrite it in your best handwriting.
5. Draw a picture of your country's flag on a piece of art paper.

Guide-Word Guides

These hiking guides will put your students on the trail to good dictionary skills! Cut out the gameboard on page 80. Have a student color the gameboard and glue it inside a folder. Cut slits at the top of the folder as shown and insert strips labeled with guide word pairs. Use the hiker pattern on page 79 to decorate the folder's cover. Make a set of game cards labeled with words that would be found between the guide word pairs. Also make bonus and hazard cards labeled with the sentences below. Provide game markers, a dictionary, and a die.

Jean O. Youngsteadt
Springfield, MO

Hazards: Attacked by swarms of mosquitoes. Go back one.
Fallen tree across trail. Lose a turn!
Poison ivy on the path. Go back one.

Bonuses: Insect repellant works. Go ahead one.
Fish are biting today. Go ahead one.
No rain in the forecast. Go ahead one.

glee – glory

glow – glut

Guide-Word Guides

Alphabet Easel

Children will get hooked on alphabetizing at this center built for two. Fold a heavy piece of poster board in half lengthwise to form a long "easel." Attach five inexpensive, press-on plastic hooks on each side of the board. Make word cards to alphabetize, punching a hole in each for hanging. The student draws five cards to hook in order. Children can work in pairs to check each other's answers.

also   alter   alternate

always

mistake

misty   miss

Jane Cuba
Redford, MI

Mouthwatering Practice

Ask your students to bring in cookbooks from home to equip a reference skills center. Post a list of favorite foods near the collection of cookbooks. During his free time, a student finds the appropriate recipes using the cookbooks' indexes. Try featuring foods which coordinate with your social studies unit or the special season of the year. As a follow-up, students might also enjoy making their own cookbook of favorite recipes, developing an accurate index.

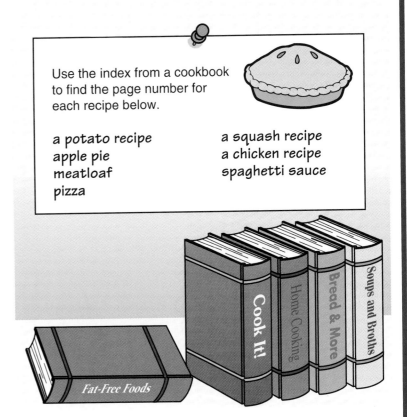

Use the index from a cookbook to find the page number for each recipe below.

a potato recipe
apple pie
meatloaf
pizza

a squash recipe
a chicken recipe
spaghetti sauce

Fishing For Facts

Reel in a line of fishy facts with this fun center idea. Collect a supply of thin, short sticks to use as fishing poles. Duplicate several copies of the fish patterns on page 81. Label each fish with a research question pertaining to a current unit of study or the interests of your students. After laminating the fish, cut them out; then punch a hole in each fish and attach it to a "pole" with a length of string. Drop the poles into a decorated bucket for easy storage. During free time, a student can reel in a question and use reference books to locate its answer.

FISHING FOR FACTS

Worth A Thousand Words

When students are stuck for a writing idea, just tell them to say, "Cheese!" Make an eye-catching "camera" by decorating a file folder as shown and stapling its sides together. Mount interesting magazine pictures on large index cards; then laminate them for durability. Store the cards in the camera. Encourage a reluctant writer to choose a picture from the camera and write a story about what's happening in the photo, what happened before the photo was snapped, or what will happen next. Change the pictures frequently for lots of picture-perfect writing opportunities.

Karoleigh K. Nitchman
Hurtsboro School Foundation
Hurtsboro, AL

Summer Reviews

Set the scene for this back-to-school writing center with stand-up displays from a local video store. Mount student directions on one of the displays as shown. Students write about their summers as if they were smash movie hits, including information about the supporting actors and actresses. Extend the activity by having students create movie posters for their silver screen hits!

Cindy Newell—Gr. 5
Washington Irving Elementary
Durant, OK

Directions

ARNOLD IN THE ACTION-ATOR

Writing Cans

My students "can it" at our creative writing center! Several General Foods® International Coffee cans, each containing five unrelated objects, are located at the center. For example, one can contains a cork, a foreign coin, a rubber band, a button, and a star cutout. Students must write stories in which each of the five objects plays a vital role. As an added challenge, the setting of the story must include the country from which the coffee is styled. For example, Cafe Vienna "canned stories" must take place in Vienna, Austria. Students research the country so that the setting is relevant to the plot. Since the cans are numbered on the bottom, students rotate and write as many different stories as there are coffee cans.

Marcia Murphy
Shawsville Middle School
Shawsville, VA

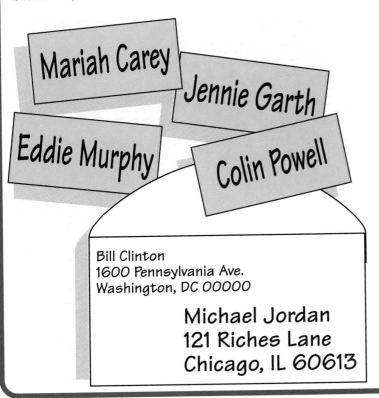

Celebrity Pen Pals

Improve your students' writing skills at this motivational center. To begin, have each student choose a different movie star, musician, or politician and write the famous person's name on a slip of paper, making sure to include his name too. Place all slips in a container; then have each student draw out one name (other than the one he wrote) to identify his celebrity pen pal. Next have each student address an envelope to his pen pal. Store these envelopes at a center. Have students write letters to their pen pals at the center, placing each in the correct envelope for delivery. Have a student deliver the letters each morning. Return the empty envelopes to the center.

Brently M. Pollard—Gr. 5
Westmont Elementary School
Martinez, GA

Greeting Card Folders

You don't have to be an artist to create attractive learning centers! Use old greeting cards to make colorful, creative writing centers. Glue the front of a greeting card on the inside of a colored file folder. List words to accompany the artwork theme of the card on the other side of the folder. Students use the words to write seasonal poems, stories, or plays. Write story starters on the back of the folder for students who need some help to begin writing.

Karen E. Morell—Learning Disabilities
Beavercreek Schools
Beavercreek, OH

Information Station

To encourage students to write letters, prepare a "freebie" information station. Each month fill the pocket on the poster with different samples of materials that can be obtained free from a company. Clip an envelope with the company's address to the bottom of the poster. A student looks through the material and writes a letter requesting information. Provide a supply of stamps that students can purchase from you so that letters can be sent immediately. Good sources of addresses are manufacturers' giveaways listed in magazines or advertised on food and toy packages. Have kids keep their eyes open for new "freebies" to add to the center.

Cathie Weaver
Wesley Christian School
Springfield, GA

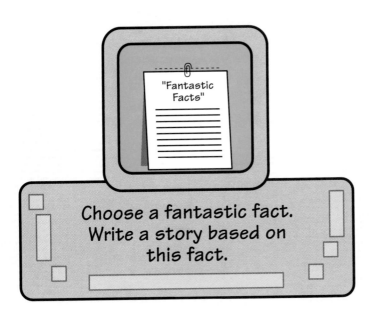

"Fantastic Facts"

Choose a fantastic fact. Write a story based on this fact.

Believe It Or Not!

Fantastic facts encourage creative writing at this center. Place a simple computer cutout (pattern on page 82) at the center, and clip a piece of paper labeled "Fantastic Facts" to the screen. Students use reference books to locate and write unusual facts on this paper. When visiting the center, a student chooses a fact from the computer screen and creates a story based on it.

Sue Nations
Sylva, NC

Lollipop, Lollipop

The following writing center is sure to be "popular" with your students. Cut out eight 3-inch circles using a differently-colored paper for each circle. On each circle write one of the color questions below, coordinating the colored circles with the color questions. Glue a tongue depressor to the back of each circle to make a "lollipop." After decorating each pop with glitter, wrap it in plastic wrap and tie the wrap with a strand of colorful yarn. Place the lollipops in a fancy basket to complete this attractive center.

List ten things that are red. Pick one item from your list and describe it without using the word "red."

- Green is supposed to be a soothing, relaxing color. Why do you think this is true?
- List ten things that are red. Pick one item from your list and describe it without using the word "red."
- Sometimes when people are sad, they say that they have the "blues." Write about a time that you had the "blues."
- Why do you suppose school buses are yellow? Write a petition requesting that the color of buses be changed. What color will you choose? What arguments will you give for using the new color?
- Brown is a very common color. List one brown thing for each letter of the alphabet.
- Write about the color purple. Tell how purple looks, smells, feels, tastes, and sounds. Use comparisons and similes.
- What would you do if you woke up one morning to find that all of your hair had turned bright pink?
- People think of a rainbow as a sign of hope or good luck. Write a story in which a rainbow signals a positive turning point in a character's life.

Karoleigh K. Nitchman, Hurtsboro School Foundation, Hurtsboro, AL

Top Secret!

What makes writing a story exciting for students? When they're able to include themselves in the plots! Let students become the detectives with this fun-filled folder activity. Glue a large, white index card labeled as shown inside a file folder. Label the outside of the folder "TOP SECRET." Store items such as the following inside:

- A magazine picture of a person, glued to an index card so that it resembles a snapshot
- An imitation credit card, labeled with its owner's name
- A variety of postcards, labeled with messages
- An index card labeled to resemble a boat or plane ticket to a specific destination
- A colorful note labeled with a person's name and telephone number

A student working on the folder first describes the person he's looking for, using the information in the folder. Then he chooses one "crime" from the folder's index card and writes a story about his case, including how he solved the crime and captured the suspect. Your kids will love these folders, so enlist parent volunteers to help you make several. In other folders, include items such as matchbook covers, cruise tickets, and menus from local restaurants.

LeVern Shan, Goliad Elementary, Odessa, TX

You are looking for:
Tim Carter

Reason (choose one):
He lost his pet roadrunner.
He borrowed a friend's false teeth.
He drew on the sidewalk.

Bermuda

Linda Smith
555-1562

7979-8432-5632
Bermuda
Whaler Card
EXP. 9/99
Tim Carter

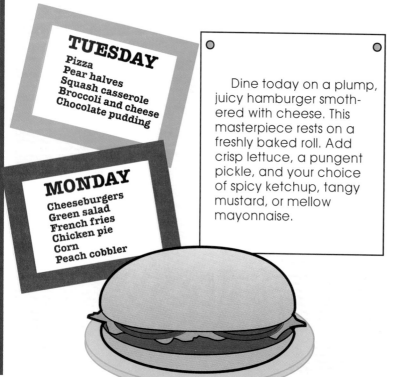

TUESDAY
Pizza
Pear halves
Squash casserole
Broccoli and cheese
Chocolate pudding

Dine today on a plump, juicy hamburger smothered with cheese. This masterpiece rests on a freshly baked roll. Add crisp lettuce, a pungent pickle, and your choice of spicy ketchup, tangy mustard, or mellow mayonnaise.

MONDAY
Cheeseburgers
Green salad
French fries
Chicken pie
Corn
Peach cobbler

Mouthwatering Menus

Don't be surprised when stomachs start to growl at this descriptive-writing center! Cut apart a copy of your school lunch menu for the week. Mount each daily menu on a colorful index card; then place the menus in a basket at a center. A student selects a daily menu and rewrites it in the form of a descriptive paragraph on a large index card. Post finished paragraphs with the daily menu on a bulletin board.

Mary Anne Haffner
Waynesboro, PA

Behind Closed Doors

Let your students make a "mysterious" creative writing center. Give each child a file folder with instructions to decorate it to look like a door. Encourage students to design (and label) specific, creative doors. How about a door to Dr. Frankenstein's laboratory, to the San Francisco 49ers' locker room, to a favorite star's dressing room? Place completed folders together at a writing center. A student can choose a "door" and write a story describing what he thinks he'd find behind it. Finished stories can be placed inside the folders for checking, then mounted on a bulletin board.

Dear Diary

If your students keep a daily or weekly journal, they may need help finding something to write about. Purchase an inexpensive journal or diary. Write a topic or story starter at the top of each page. Place the journal in a convenient spot in your room. When a student needs a topic to write about, let her look through the journal. When she finds an idea that interests her, she signs her name on the page below the topic. When she uses the journal again, the student will be able to see which topics she's already written about. Use the topics listed below for starters.

Sports I Like
My Favorite Holiday
I Get Angry When…
The Subject I Like Best
When I'm Sick
Things I Treasure
The Funniest Story
Things I Celebrate
My Biggest Worry
Things I Would Change

It's O.K. To Lose
What I Like About Me
Why I Need Friends
Does Fighting Make Sense?
I Laugh When…
Things I'm Glad About
You Can't Always Be Perfect
Once I Dreamed…
Things I'd Do Again
My Favorite Animal

Pencil P-O-W-E-R!

Students practice the P-O-W-E-R plan of creative writing (Plan, Organize, Write, Evaluate, Rewrite) at this center. Place several items of interest in the center. Attach a note card to each item that states a situation, a question, or an unfinished story relating to the item (see the examples below). Provide writing paper, construction paper, tagboard patterns, a hole punch, and yarn at the center for students to make story booklets. Change the center items frequently and include seasonal objects when possible. Students will find that anything can be transformed into an exciting writing motivator! Display completed stories for others to read.

Sample items and note cards:

  old sneaker—"You wouldn't believe where I have been in the last 24 hours! First I…"

  pair of sunglasses—Cindy spent the last of her allowance on a pair of sunglasses instead of going to a movie. List five reasons why you think she made this choice; then tell what you would have done.

  pencil—You are taking a test and your pencil whispers that you have made a mistake.

  star—What superstar would you like to be? How would this change your life?

Cindy Newell—Gr. 5
Washington Irving Elementary
Durant, OK

Here Lies…

Honor favorite book and story characters at this writing center. Enlarge the tombstone pattern on page 83 and label it with the directions shown. Post the tombstone at a center equipped with a tagboard copy of the pattern on page 83, gray construction paper, and scissors. Cover a wall with your students' creative epitaphs for a spooky display.

Sr. Ann Claire Rhoads
Mother Seton School
Emmitsburg, MD

R.I.P.

Directions:

1. Choose a character from a book, story, or myth you have recently read.
2. On your paper, write an epitaph for your character. An *epitaph* is an inscription on a tombstone in memory of the person buried there.
3. Proofread and correct your epitaph.
4. Use the pattern to trace a tombstone onto gray paper. Cut it out and copy your epitaph on it.

Example: *Here lies Old Yeller*
That old, yellow hound.
A braver dog
Will never be found!

Ads For The Future

Imagine what the classified ads will look like in the year 2500! What jobs will be available? What new products or old antiques will be for sale? Get students pondering these questions with this future-thinking writing center. Cover a small bulletin board at a center with newsprint. Add the title "Classified Ads Of The Future." Place writing paper, catalogs, and copies of classifieds at the center. Have students write ads for antique ten-speed bicycles, robots for rent, space stations, etc. Post the students' ads on a bulletin board for entertaining reading.

Michelle Martin
Macon, GA

Create A Filmstrip

Here's how:
1. Cut a piece of adding machine tape eight inches long.
2. With a pencil, draw parallel lines one inch apart for the length of the tape. Then draw in one-inch frames.
3. With a pencil, write and illustrate a story in the frames. Then trace over the words and illustrations with markers.
4. Put the filmstrip where your teacher asked you to.

More filmstrip ideas:
1. Record the audio for the filmstrip before showing.
2. Use rhythm instruments to signal the projectionist to change frames.
3. Store filmstrips in empty film canisters.
4. Let students check out filmstrips for small-group or individual viewing.
5. Set up a filmstrip learning center and have questions to accompany the strip to be viewed.
6. Pop some popcorn and have a filmstrip festival.

Create A Filmstrip

This center is fun, versatile, and low in cost. Just gather the following supplies and prepare the directions; then let your students jump into action!

Center supplies:

adding machine tape	rulers
pencils	scissors
fine-point markers	

Additional supplies needed:
liquid cooking oil
container for soaking filmstrips
paper towels

After the children have completed the center, soak the filmstrips in cooking oil until saturated. Wipe off excess oil with paper towels, and let the filmstrips dry overnight. To view, pull each strip carefully through the projector, frame by frame. Take extra care not to bend the strip.

Linda Christian Allgeier
Deep Springs Elementary
Lexington, KY

Cloudy Daze

"What if…." All children play this day-dreaming game, so why not tap those wonderings for some good creative thinking and writing? Write each of the situations listed below on a construction paper cloud. Punch a hole at the top of each cloud, add yarn, and attach the cutout to a coat hanger to make a mobile. A student picks a cloud and writes a paragraph suggesting how to handle the situation. Students selecting the same situation may want to lead a class discussion on the merits and pitfalls of both of their solutions.

— The principal asks you to take charge of the entire school for a day.
— Someone delivers 69 crates of ripe tomatoes to your house.
— While fishing in a pond near your home, you hook an alligator.
— You are accused of a crime you didn't commit.
— You break out in a rash from head to toe on your doctor's day off.
— You inherit a million dollars with the condition that you spend it in 24 hours or lose it all.
— You are awakened at your school desk only to be told that you've been asleep for six weeks!

No Experience Necessary

Project students into the future with this writing center. Place a copy of the employment classifieds from your local newspaper at a center. After a careful examination, a student visiting the center chooses a job he would like to have. Next he writes a "Dear Prospective Employer" letter expressing his interest in the job and giving the qualifications he has that will make him a good choice for employment. Place completed letters in a file folder labeled "Applicants." Allow other students to read the letters and respond to them as if they were the prospective employers.

Janice Scott—Gr. 5
Rockport Elementary
Rockport, TX

Mail Call!

With just a little bit of time, you can make a functional writing center that will provide hours of writing practice. Mount two pieces of poster board on cardboard. Duplicate the mailbox pattern on page 84. After coloring and cutting out the pattern, glue it on one of the poster board sheets as shown. Tape the two sheets together on the back with wide masking or packing tape to make a standing study carrel. Attach student directions and sample letters. Cut a slit in the mailbox where shown and fill with letter-writing task cards (see the list below). Provide a supply of envelopes. Place a box labeled "Post Office" near the carrel so that students can "mail" their finished letters to the teacher.

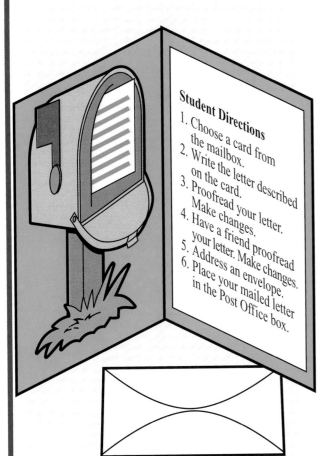

Student Directions
1. Choose a card from the mailbox.
2. Write the letter described on the card.
3. Proofread your letter. Make changes.
4. Have a friend proofread your letter. Make changes.
5. Address an envelope.
6. Place your mailed letter in the Post Office box.

Task Cards
- **Business Letter:** Ask a travel agency to send you brochures describing tourist spots on Jupiter.
- **Letter of Condolence:** Send a note of sympathy to your dog for his bad case of fleas.
- **Thank-you Letter:** Thank your aunt for her birthday gift—a toothbrush with no bristles.
- **Invitation:** Invite the President of the United States to your next slumber party.
- **Congratulations:** Send a letter of congratulations to your friend who was just given a telephone for his bedroom.
- **Business Letter:** Write to a shoe company and order a pair of sneakers for your pet orangutan.
- **Friendly Letter:** You've just realized that you've become invisible. Write a letter to one of your parents telling how this happened.

Current Events Photo Album

Make a little news with a terrific current events learning center. Label an inexpensive photo album "Current Events Yearbook." Keep the album at a center with a supply of small index cards. Each week place a newspaper article about a current event on a page in the album. During free time, a student reads the week's article; then he writes his opinion about the event on an index card and places it below the article (or on the following page if more space is needed). With all that writing and current events practice, this is a center that packs a double punch!

Local Man Saves Life

Middle School Gets Grant

Sr. Ann Claire Rhoads
St. Pius X School
Greensboro, NC

Mary Anne couldn't believe her ears. Was it really Bobby Brown on the phone? Mary Anne...

He was the most unusual patient Doc Blake had ever seen. He was covered with purple dots from head to toe. Dr. Blake...

I first became suspicious when my grandmother picked me up riding a motorcycle! She...

Cliff-Hangers

What kid doesn't love a good nail-biting, on-the-edge-of-your-seat cliff-hanger? To make your own cliff-hanger center, fold a three-foot-long piece of colored paper over the bottom bar of a colorful plastic coat hanger. Staple the paper so that it hangs from the hanger. At the top of the paper, start a story, leaving the last sentence unfinished; then hang the hanger at a center. During free time a student can continue the cliff-hanger story, leaving his last sentence unfinished for the next writer. At the end of the week, read the completed tale as a class; then let students illustrate it. Display the finished cliff-hanger and illustrations in a hallway.

Sheryl Poffinbarger
Dellview Elementary
San Antonio, TX

Give Me A Start

Students stumped for writing ideas? My writing center includes three small manila envelopes labeled *Beginning, Middle,* and *End.* Each envelope contains ideas that students can use to help them develop their stories. Whenever a student gets writer's block, he pulls a labeled index card from each envelope. The skeleton of the story is provided; the student then gets to add the juicy details! Some of my examples include:

Beginning: *One very dark and stormy night.... Sally was so out of breath, she had to stop.*

Middle: *He looked surprised and started his plan. The package was bigger than she imagined it would be.*

End: *It was all going to work out after all. When they got home, they promised....*

Kathleen Jordan
Orange County Schools
Altamonte Springs, FL

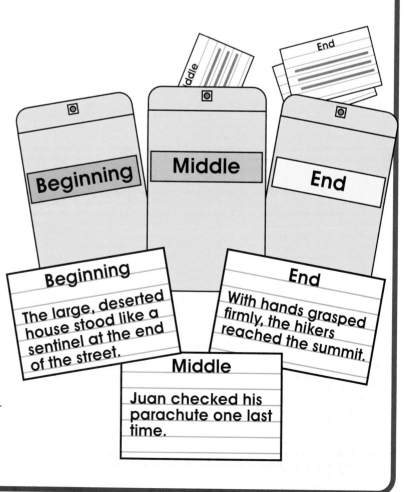

Beginning

Middle

End

Beginning
The large, deserted house stood like a sentinel at the end of the street.

End
With hands grasped firmly, the hikers reached the summit.

Middle
Juan checked his parachute one last time.

You Can't Win Them All!

Score points with this newspaper activity. Provide the sports sections of various newspapers at a center. Have students find articles that include team scores. Each student chooses a story and rewrites it from the point of view of a fan or a member of the losing team. Display the new versions with the original stories, along with sports photos and posters at the center.

Janice Scott—Gr. 5
Rockport Elementary
Rockport, TX

Star Quality

Set up a fan mail center for loads of motivating letter-writing practice. Have students brainstorm a list of favorite music, movie, and television stars. Obtain addresses for as many of the stars as possible through supermarket fan magazines or other sources suggested by your school's librarian. Post the addresses at a center equipped with stationery, envelopes, and stamps. While visiting the center, students can write letters requesting pictures or information about their favorite stars.

Janice Scott—Gr. 5
Rockport Elementary
Rockport, TX

Eva Davidson
3868-A West Ave.
Greensboro, NC 27407

Whitney Houston
1000 Big Star Avenue
Los Angeles, CA 34021

Keesha Teal
2001 Meadowood Rd.
Beaumont, TX 00000

Will Smith
119 Hollywood Hills
Los Angeles, CA 34022

Laughing Limericks

Instead of cluttering up your idea file, put humorous magazine and newspaper clippings to good use. Place this folder activity at a creative writing center. (See the porcupine and zebra patterns on page 85.) Good possibilities for other activity folders include riddles, cartoons, comic strips, and tongue twisters. (Hint: Greeting cards are another great source of humor!)

1. Study the limericks. Notice the rhyming and syllable patterns.
2. Try to write a limerick using the same rhyming and syllable patterns.
   Remember:
   • five lines
   • first, second, and last lines rhyme
   • Aim for a syllable pattern of 8-8-5-5-8.

Try these for starters:
   • Miss Centipede says, "I'll admit…
   • (rhyming words: fit, bit, hit, kit, lit, mitt, sit, etc.)

   • A happy-go-lucky young guy…
   (rhyming words: fly, by, try, dye, why, shy, buy, cry, lie, etc.)

   • A beaver's best friend is his tail…
   (rhyming words: dale, fail, hail, gale, jail, mail, male, snail, pail, wail, etc.)

This porcupine says, "When I'm sickly,
I try to get well very quickly.
Because my sweet nurse
Says there's nothing worse
Than rubbing down someone so prickly!"

I sometimes have problems I find,
In dressing the way I'm inclined.
Those polka-dot types
Don't go with my stripes.
But still they're my favorite kinds!

Having A Great Time! Wish You Were Here!

Want to keep in touch over the summer? Students will want to write to school chums and drop you a line after completing this file folder activity. Provide blank 4" x 7" index cards. Have each student plan an imaginary trip to any place in the world and design a picture postcard from this vacation spot. Use travel brochures, magazine pictures, and posters to encourage daydreaming. Place the postcards in a file folder pocket with a list of student names and addresses. A student chooses a postcard, writes a message on the back, addresses the card, and drops it in a classroom mailbox.

Name	Address

Choose a postcard destination.

Fill in your name and address.
Write to the person above your name.

Help Me Out!

Since kids love to look at photos of themselves and their classmates, I take pictures of my students working in cooperative groups, participating in special events, or discovering new things on field trips. I display the pictures on the outside of our classroom door for a while; then I store them in a large envelope labeled "Help Me Out! Album Pix." When a student has extra time, she places the pictures in an album and adds a caption for the activity featured. Parents love to look at our album when they visit the classroom.

Catherine Jarratt—Grs. 4–6
Woodside School
Topsham, ME

Magical Mythmakers

Like other special types of stories, a myth has certain characteristics all its own. After reading and discussing several myths, give students an opportunity to create their own mythological masterpieces. Enlarge, color, and cut out the Pegasus pattern on page 85; then mount it on a piece of poster board. Add a cut-out cloud and a pocket as shown. In the pocket, store index cards labeled with the myth ideas listed below. Provide art supplies for students' drawings as well. Display the finished myths and pictures in a student-made "Myth Magazine."

Patricia L. Turner
Bismarck, ND

MAGICAL MYTH-MAKERS

Be sure your myth:
- Includes at least one godlike character.
- Explains why things in nature are as they are.

Choose a card and write a myth. Draw a picture of your animal as it looks in your myth.

How did the turtle get its shell?

Myth Ideas
How did the turtle get its shell?
How did the giraffe get its long neck?
How did the lion get its roar?
How did the rabbit get its fluffy tail?
How did the elephant get its trunk?
How did the cat get its meow?
How did the kangaroo get its pouch?
How did the skunk get its scent?

MATH

Graph It!

Get students into the center-making act! Ask each child to bring in a graph from a newspaper or magazine. (*USA Today* is an excellent source of easy-to-read, interesting graphs.) Have each student mount his graph onto a piece of construction paper that's large enough for the graph and several questions. Instruct each student (with the help of his cooperative teammates or a partner, if desired) to write two or more questions about his graph and their answers on scrap paper. After proofreading, have the child copy his questions onto the front of the card and the answers on the back. Laminate the cards for durability; then place them in a box at a center. Keep a supply of newspapers, magazines, construction paper, glue, scissors, and markers at the center so students can add to your graph card collection.

Helen M. Hargett—Grs. 4–6
Darlington Middle School
Rome, GA

Nancy L. Martin—Gr. 4
Allen Jay Elementary
High Point, NC

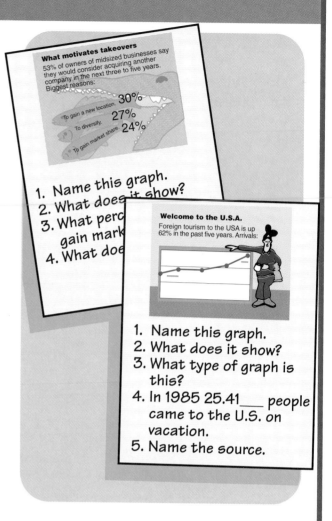

What motivates takeovers
53% of owners of midsized businesses say they would consider acquiring another company in the next three to five years. Biggest reasons:
To gain a new location. 30%
To diversify. 27%
To gain market share. 24%

1. Name this graph.
2. What does it show?
3. What perc...
gain mark...
4. What doe...

Welcome to the U.S.A.
Foreign tourism to the USA is up 62% in the past five years. Arrivals:

1. Name this graph.
2. What does it show?
3. What type of graph is this?
4. In 1985 25.41___ people came to the U.S. on vacation.
5. Name the source.

SITTING PRETTY

Spin the spinner; then write and solve each math problem on your paper. Have a partner check your work.

×24 ÷2
÷6   ×9

1. 82
2. 456
3. 303
4. 271
5. 93
6. 79
7. 163
8. 34
9. 123
10. 29
11. 90
12. 611
13. 46
14. 450
15. 33

Sitting Pretty

Your students will go nuts over this colorful center—and you'll love its versatility too! Duplicate page 86 and have a student color it. Mount the page on a slightly larger piece of construction paper; then laminate it. Use a wipe-off marker to program each nut with a number and each section of the spinner with an operation/number. Provide a paper clip so students can use it with a pencil to make a spinner as shown on page 10. When you're ready to change the center, simply wipe the nuts and spinner clean and reprogram. Later in the year, program the center with fractions or decimals.

①
1. On what date was this order taken?
2. How many cinnamon rolls were ordered?
3. What was the subtotal?
4. If five people ordered this meal, what would be the total cost?

CHRISTIE'S CINNAMON ROLL HOUSE

ROLLS   3.39
  10 ITEMS
TAX   .17
TOTAL   3.56
CASH   3.60
CHANGE   .04

OPER. 1
11-10-96   4:53PM

Save Those Receipts!

The next time you go shopping or eat at a fast-food restaurant, hang on to your receipts! In a snap, you can transform them into hours of math practice. Glue each receipt to a colored index card. On the card, write several questions for the student to answer on his own paper or a duplicated answer sheet. Number the cards and provide an answer key. Build your collection of activity cards by asking students and parents to save receipts for you!

Super Bowl Season

You can bet you'll score big with students when you put this folder game at your math center! Draw a simple football field inside a folder as shown. Cut two footballs from a laminated sheet of brown construction paper for markers. For quick and easy game cards, glue one or more math worksheets onto a sheet of tagboard. Laminate the sheet; then cut the math problems apart. Provide an answer key or write answers on the backs of the problems with a wipe-off marker. Store the game markers and problems in a pocket attached to the back of the folder.

For two players:
1. Put your marker at Start.
2. Draw a problem and solve it on your paper. Check the key.
3. If correct, move 10 yards. If incorrect, do not move.
4. First to reach TOUCHDOWN wins.

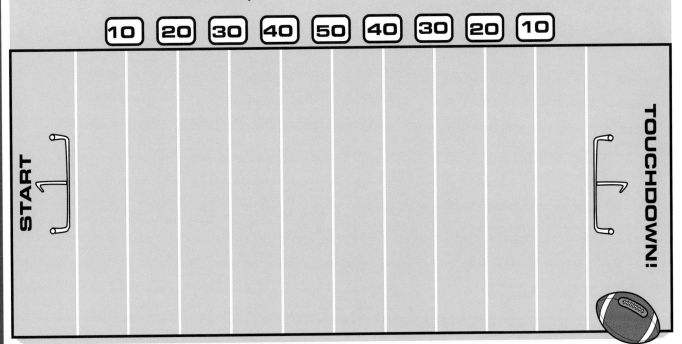

10 20 30 40 50 40 30 20 10

START

TOUCHDOWN!

Auto Mart

Everyone—even kids—loves new cars, so why not put that interest to good use? Cut out automobile ads from newspapers and magazines. Make sure that each ad shows a picture, price, and description of the vehicle. Paste each ad on a posterboard card. Program the back of the card with math or language questions concerning the ad. Laminate the cards for durability. These activity cards are terrific for review and as freetime fillers.

Pamela Mckedy—Resource Teacher
Highland Falls Middle School
Highland Falls, NY

For A Limited Time Only

88 Mazda 929
Only $12,050.⁰⁰

FEATURES
- Automatic.
- Cloth Interior
- Tilt Steering Wheel
- Red W/Red Interior
- Power Windows
- 30,000 Miles
- And Much, Much More

1. If you made a down payment of $3,500.00, how much would you still owe on the car?

2. You've just found out that you can buy an older Mazda for half the cost of this model. How much does the older model cost?

2/12

Surf's Up!

1/4   1/2   1/3   2/3   1/6   3/4

2/8

Surf's Up!

Surf's up for fraction practice! Duplicate the cover art on page 87; then color and glue it to the front of a file folder. Glue another folder inside this folder. Label the inside of the folder as shown and cut slits where indicated by the dotted lines. Write matching equivalent fractions on tongue depressor "surfboards" for students to place in the slits. Provide an answer key and a pocket for surfboard storage on the back.

Sneaker Sale

Nike. $65
Air Jordan. . . $75
Addidas. $60
Reebok. $60
Cougar. $55

Sneaker Sale

Sneaker season is any season! But just how expensive are those popular treads? Have students brainstorm a list of favorite sneakers; then have them investigate catalogs and local shoe stores to find out the prices. List this information on a chart displayed at your math center. Have students use this information to write story problems about their favorite sneakers.

Once the story problems have been written and proofread, place them in a pair of high-topped sneakers at the center. A student visiting the center chooses five problems, solves them on her paper, and then places her work in a shoe box. Award a pair of shoelaces to the student who scores the highest marks at this center.

Sweet Treats

Count on a jarful of tempting cookies to provide plenty of sweet place-value practice! Duplicate page 88. Glue it to a sheet of construction paper; then have a student volunteer color it. After laminating the sheet, use a wipe-off marker to program each cookie with a number that contains an underlined digit. A student using the center numbers his paper 1–12; then he writes the place value of each underlined digit. Reprogram the center simply by wiping it clean and labeling it with new numbers.

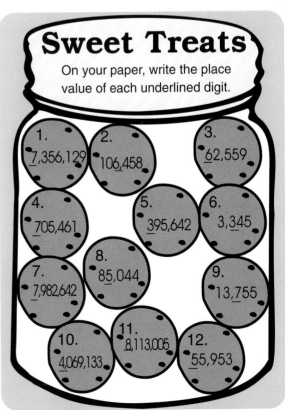

Sweet Treats

On your paper, write the place value of each underlined digit.

1. 7,356,12<u>9</u>
2. 106,4<u>5</u>8
3. <u>6</u>2,559
4. <u>7</u>05,461
5. 395,6<u>4</u>2
6. 3,3<u>4</u>5
7. 7,<u>9</u>82,642
8. 85,0<u>4</u>4
9. 13,<u>7</u>55
10. 4,0<u>6</u>9,133
11. 8,113,00<u>5</u>
12. 55,9<u>5</u>3

MATH

Baseball Card Math

"Take me out to the ball game" and to a great math center that's packed with student appeal! Place team sets of baseball cards at a center, along with a poster labeled with problem-solving tasks and a calculator. Let students work in pairs at the center to complete the tasks. Or divide the class into several teams. Give a set of cards and a list of the tasks to each team. Whichever way you use them, baseball cards are a great way to score a math home run!

Baseball Card Tasks
Choose a team set of cards and complete three of these activities.

- List the players in order from the youngest to the oldest.
- Find the average age of the team's players.
- List the players in order according to batting averages, beginning with the player who has the highest batting average.
- Find the team's average batting average.
- Find the difference between the highest and lowest batting averages on the team.
- Find the total weight of the team.
- Find the average weight of the team members.
- Find the total number of home runs (or triples, doubles, or singles) hit by the team during a specific year listed on the cards.

Kari Koebernick—Gr. 5
Enders-Salk School
Schaumburg, IL

Math Fold-Aways

Program these fold-away math manipulatives—that resemble plastic photo or credit card holders—to practice a variety of skills. Cut a supply of four-inch squares from poster board. Program sets of three squares with a math problem, the correct answer, and an incorrect answer. Place the squares in a row (with the question in the center) on Con-Tact® adhesive covering or laminating film, leaving about 1/2" between the squares. Then cover the front of the cards with another piece of adhesive covering. Trim the outside edges; then place a self-sticking dot on the back of the correct-answer square. A student visiting the math center chooses a fold-away, solves the problem on his paper, and then folds back the incorrect answer. Program additional fold-aways to practice with synonyms, vocabulary, and other skills.

Rebecca Gibson Baker—Gr. 4
Edward Bell School
Camp Hill, AL

Math Challenge!

These skill cards challenge students to master math facts. Prepare sets of cards for various math skills. Write 30 math facts, with no answers, on each card. Color-code the card sets according to skill. Laminate each card for durability. Store the sets in Zip-Loc® bags. Provide a one-minute timer, color-coded answer keys, and these student instructions: Pick a card. Practice saying the answers out loud with a study buddy. See if you can say the answers in 60 seconds or less.

Mary Anne T. Haffner
Waynesboro, PA

Shave And A Haircut

Shave And A Haircut

A friendly race between two barbers turns math practice into a fun game. Duplicate the gameboard on page 89. After a student volunteer colors and cuts it out, glue the gameboard inside a file folder. Label a set of cut-out cards with math problems. Write the answers on the backs of the cards. Store the cards, two game markers, and a coin in a pocket attached to the back of the folder. Adapt the folder to any skill by providing a new set of game cards.

Jean O. Youngsteadt
Springfield, MO

MATH

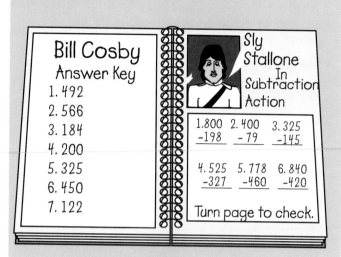

Album Of The Stars

All you need to make this versatile center are a magnetic photo album, some math worksheets, and your students' favorite stars! Ask students to bring in magazine and newspaper photos of famous entertainment personalities. Cut the worksheets in halves or thirds. Mount one of the "mini-sheets" with a photo on a right-hand page of the album. Add a clever caption, if desired. Place an answer key on the next page. A student can flip to his favorite star's page, complete the problems on his own paper, then turn the page to check his work.

How Do You Eat Your Jumly?

A spoonful of Jumly makes this graphing center a tasty treat! Duplicate page 90. Color each wedge of the circle graph a different color; also color the worksheet. Cut out both items and glue them inside a file folder as shown. Write the answer key on the back of the folder.

Sylvia McFeaters
Slippery Rock, PA

Answer Key
1. 11%
2. from the can
3. on asparagus
4. 31%
5. 35%
6. 22
7. 24
8. 38

Practice The Facts!

1. 30÷5=
2. 42÷7=
3. 24÷3=
4. 36÷6=
5. 54÷9=
6. 16÷2=
7. 72÷8=
8. 28÷4=
9. 21÷3=
10. 40÷5=

Chalkboard Learning Centers

Turn a spare chalkboard into an instant learning center. Label several 3″ x 9″ tagboard cards with a skill you are currently studying, writing answers on the back. Add a cute sticker to decorate each card. Next loop a piece of yarn through a hole punched at the top of each card. Attach one or two cards to the chalkboard with magnets. During free time, a student goes to the center, chooses a card, writes his answers on the chalkboard, and turns the card over to check his work. Your students will love the chance to write on the board, and you'll love the learning that takes place!

Kathleen Jones—Gr. 4
Anna Jarvis Elementary
Grafton, WV

Coupon Clippers

Get your scissors ready and clip some coupons for this real-life math center! Ask students to bring unwanted coupons to school. Duplicate and color the cash register pattern on page 91. Cut out the pattern and glue it inside a folder. Attach a paper pocket to the cash register as shown; then fill it with a cash register tape from a grocery store and several coupons. A student using this center finds the total savings of the coupons and then subtracts it from the sales receipt total. Place an answer key in a pocket attached to the back of the folder. Change the coupons and cash register tapes frequently to provide lots of practice. Reward smart shoppers with coupons good for special free-time activities or classroom privileges.

Coupon Clippers

Find the total savings of the coupons in the cash register. Then subtract them from the sales receipt. Check your answer using the key.

$0,000,000.00

This Week's Coupons & Receipts

25¢ When You Buy Two

10¢

DOWNY

10¢

35¢

AJAX

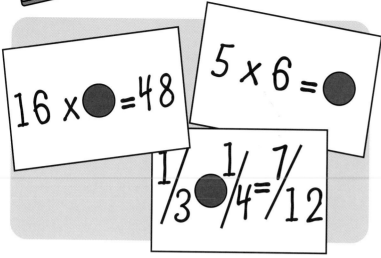

Math Trees

Adapt these versatile, student-made math trees to reinforce skills at any time of the year!

Materials needed for each group:

four 12-inch-long pieces of string (per student)
4 small paper cups (per student)
hole puncher
scissors
large container (plastic bucket, clay pot, etc.)
enough sand to fill the large container
colorful construction paper
tree limb
ruler
marker
pen or pencil
glue or tape

How to make:

1. Decorate the large container with colorful paper. Position the tree limb in the container; then fill the container with sand to keep the limb upright.
2. Have each group member cut four one-inch squares of construction paper and punch a hole in one corner of each square.
3. Instruct each student to turn his four paper cups bottom-side up and write a math problem (without an answer) on the side of each cup.
4. Have each student use a pen or pencil point to poke two small holes in the bottom of each cup.
5. Have the student—beginning from the outside—thread a piece of string through one hole of a cup, through a paper square, then back through the second hole in the cup. Then have him tie the two ends together and repeat this step with his other three cups.
6. Instruct students to write the matching answers for their math problems on the paper squares. Then have them pull the outer end of each loop until the answer is hidden inside the cup.
7. Have the group hang its cups from the tree limb.

Encourage students to visit the trees and solve their classmates' problems. To reveal an answer, a student simply pulls down the paper square inside the cup.

Vicki Smith, Murfreesboro, TN

"Dots" So Simple!

All you need to make this simple math center is a stack of index cards, a marker, and a supply of colorful sticky dots. Write a math problem as shown on a card, using a sticky dot in place of an important part of the problem, such as the answer, the operation symbol, an addend, etc. Write the missing element on the back of the card. Laminate the cards; then place them at your math center for practice "dots" fun for kids and easy for you!

Shady Business

Take cover for division practice! Duplicate two copies of page 92. Have a student volunteer color both pages and then trim and glue them inside a file folder as shown. Draw and color a sun at the top corner of the folder as shown. Laminate the folder; then use a wipe-off marker to label each umbrella with a number. Cut a slit in the sun and insert a paper clip. Clip an answer key to the back of the folder. Each week clip a new number card on the sun to provide lots of division practice.

Decimal Deli Delights

Give students practice adding and ordering decimals with this deli delight! Decorate the inside of a folder as shown. Write the answer key on the back of the folder. Remind students to line up the decimal points before adding. For additional practice in rounding, instruct students to round each decimal to the nearest tenth before adding.

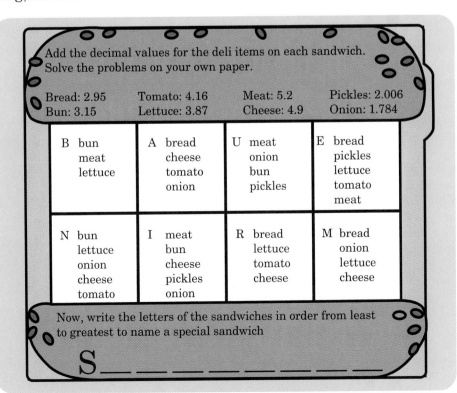

Add the decimal values for the deli items on each sandwich. Solve the problems on your own paper.

Bread: 2.95　　Tomato: 4.16　　Meat: 5.2　　Pickles: 2.006
Bun: 3.15　　Lettuce: 3.87　　Cheese: 4.9　　Onion: 1.784

B bun meat lettuce	A bread cheese tomato onion	U meat onion bun pickles	E bread pickles lettuce tomato meat
N bun lettuce onion cheese tomato	I meat bun cheese pickles onion	R bread lettuce tomato cheese	M bread onion lettuce cheese

Now, write the letters of the sandwiches in order from least to greatest to name a special sandwich

S _____ _____ _____ _____ _____ _____ _____ _____ _____

Answer Key
B. 12.22
A. 13.794
U. 12.14
E. 18.186
N. 17.864
I. 17.04
R. 15.88
M. 13.504

SUBMARINE

Edible Estimation

This mouthwatering math center will motivate your students to learn about estimation. Your center will need a balance scale and a handful of small paper clips. For each student, provide a copy of the worksheet on page 93 and a sandwich bag containing the following items: one peanut (in its shell), one Gummy Bear®, one Skittle® candy, one large marshmallow, one jelly bean, and one Mini Oreo®. Let the students know that one small paper clip is equal to about one gram of weight. Have students follow the worksheet directions to estimate, weigh, and compare their findings. Have them record their data on the record sheet. Let each student eat the contents of his baggy as a reward for completing the center.

Brenda H. McGee—Gr. 4
Meadows Elementary School
Plano, TX

Broken Hearts

Mending broken hearts is the task at this equivalents center! Decorate and label the inside of a folder as shown. Attach a spinner to each heart wheel. Cut out a supply of paper hearts; then cut half of the hearts in two. Store the hearts and heart halves in a zippered plastic bag that is clipped to the folder. Provide a chart of equivalents to use as an answer key.

To play this game for two, a player spins each wheel. If he spins two numbers that are equivalent, he earns a heart. If he spins a "heartache" (two numbers that aren't equivalent), he earns a broken heart half. A player may exchange five heart halves for one whole heart. The winner has the most hearts after each player has taken ten turns.

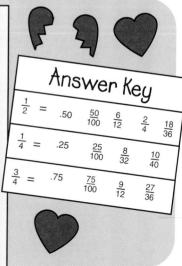

Game for two players:
1. In turn, spin each spinner.
2. If the fractions or decimals are equivalent, take a heart.
3. If the fractions or decimals are not equivalent, take a broken heart. You may exchange five broken hearts for a whole heart.
4. Be sure to check your answers with the key.
5. The winner has the most hearts after 10 spins.

Broken Hearts

Answer Key

$\frac{1}{2}$	=	.50	$\frac{50}{100}$	$\frac{6}{12}$	$\frac{2}{4}$	$\frac{18}{36}$
$\frac{1}{4}$	=	.25	$\frac{25}{100}$	$\frac{8}{32}$	$\frac{10}{40}$	
$\frac{3}{4}$	=	.75	$\frac{75}{100}$	$\frac{9}{12}$	$\frac{27}{36}$	

Chilly Challenge

Improve thinking skills with an analogies folder. For easy construction, duplicate and color the worksheet on page 93; then glue it inside a colorful folder as shown. Write the answer key on the back of the folder. To decorate the center further, glue small white paper doilies or coasters on the front and inside the folder.

Janis Ludwig
Battle Creek, MI

Think how the first two words are related. On your paper, write a word that relates to the third word in the same way. The first one's been done for you. (Hint: The colon between two words means "is related to.") Check using the answer key.

Answers:

1. large	6. ocean
2. acorn	7. leg
3. depth	8. clock
4. mother	9. dentist
5. airplane	10. end

Answer to riddle: A cold medal

Think Or Sink!

For a quick and easy thinking skills center, duplicate page 94. After having a student color the page for you, glue it to a sheet of construction paper and laminate it. Display the miniposter at a center for students to work on during free time. Post students' answers on a bulletin board titled "Great Thinkers, Inc."

THINK OR SINK!

Put on your thinking cap! Choose a question to answer. Write and illustrate your answer.

1. If you could add one day to every week, what would you name that day? Why would you choose that name?
2. What animal would make the greatest best friend? Explain your answer.
3. Besides brushing your teeth, what else can a toothbrush be used for?
4. List some words that make beautiful sounds.
5. Think of five uses for an old sneaker.
6. What do you suppose the president of the United States wore on Halloween when he was a kid?
7. What is the most useless thing in your bedroom right now? Explain your answer.
8. Design a way to wash dishes while lying down (no dishwasher allowed).
9. If you could read the mind of anyone in the world, whose mind would you choose and why?
10. Describe a recent meal without including the names of any foods or drinks.
11. You are interviewing your hero but can only ask him or her five questions. What questions would you ask?
12. Describe an event you never want to forget.
13. "A penny saved is a penny earned." Would you rather save money or spend it? Why?
14. A genie has just told you that you can trade places with anyone in the world for an hour. Who would you absolutely *not* want to trade places with? Why?

Critical Thinking Cards

Preparing a critical thinking center is a simple task with the reproducible activity cards on pages 95–98. Duplicate the cards; then mount them on construction paper before laminating and cutting them apart. Place the cards in an empty fish bowl. Attach a sign that reads "Dive In!" To help students keep track of their writing, give each child a blank file folder in which to store his work. Each time he completes one of the activities, have the student write the number of the card on a self-sticking label and stick it to the inside of his folder. Initial the label after you've reviewed the student's work.

States-And-Capitals Concentration

Use this easy-to-make center to reinforce a variety of skills and subjects throughout the year. Number 24 library book pockets from 1–24. Arrange these in grid fashion on a small bulletin board as shown. Next program 24 small index cards with the names of 12 states and their capitals. Place the capital cards in pockets 1–12 and the state cards in 13–24 in scrambled order. Provide an answer key.

The game is played by two students or teams. Each player, in turn, chooses a card from the left side and tries to match it with a card from the right side. If the two cards match, the player keeps the cards and continues play. If the two cards don't match, they are placed back into their pockets, and the next player tries. Play continues until all cards are gone. Adapt this game to other skills such as world capitals/countries, multiplication or division facts, roman/arabic numerals, terms/definitions, and antonyms/synonyms.

Where In The World?

My students don't even know they're practicing with this fun center. I post a world map on a wall with the title "Where In The World Is ____?" On Monday, I fill in the title with the name of a city. Each child must find the place on the map and identify its country, continent, hemisphere, and latitude and longitude coordinates. Each student writes his answers on a slip of paper and places it in a box. On Friday afternoon, we find out exactly "where in the world" such exotic sounding cities as Shanghai and Buenos Aires are located. Each student with all responses correct earns a bonus 100% score in social studies for the week. As an extra incentive, draw one slip from the correct responses and award the winner a small treat.

Linda Strong—Gr. 4, Celina K–8 School, Celina, TN

Our Stupendous States

Turn your students into state experts with a fun social studies center. Display the following poster at a center, along with a list of the 50 states, resource books, and 8" x 10" sheets of tagboard. To insure that no state is left out, have each student select two to research; then assign any remaining states to volunteers. After the state cutouts are finished, students can arrange them on a clothesline in alphabetical order or in order according to size, population, or date admitted to the union. Students can also group the states according to geographical region. With all this student participation, this center can't help but be successful!

Timothy J. Torrence—Gr. 5
Warsaw, IN

OUR STUPENDOUS STATES

1. Write your name by the two states you'd like to study (one student per state).

2. Trace or draw your states on tagboard. Cut them out.

3. Research your states. Look for such facts as your states' population, size, capitals, nicknames, industry, agriculture, etc. Write your information on your state cutouts.

4. Clip your finished states on the clothesline.

STATE FLOWER
Apple Blossom

The 25th State

ARKANSAS

DIAMOND STATE

27th in size

STATE TREE: PINE

Almost 2 1/2 million people

Land Of Opportunity

News Datelines

Help children to discover places in the news with datelines that tell where news stories originate. Search through newspapers and cut out datelines from around the world. Mount these inside a file folder to illustrate international, national, regional, and local datelines. Write the tasks shown inside the folder. Laminate the folder to protect it from newsprint fingerprints. Place the folder, duplicated world maps, and stacks of old newspapers at a center.

Kathy M. Peterson
Alpha, IL

International Datelines
(from someplace outside the United States)

National Datelines
(from someplace inside the United States)

Regional Datelines
(from our state and surrounding area)

Local Datelines
(from our city, town, or county)

Complete one of these activities:
1. Find and cut out the national datelines from at least 10 states. Paste the datelines on paper and write the state they are each from.

2. Find international datelines from these continents: South America, Europe, Asia, and Africa. Cut out the datelines and glue them onto the correct continent on a world map.

3. Write a news article with a dateline from your town.

4. Pretend you are a foreign correspondent for a major news agency. Choose any dateline, and write a news story from that country.

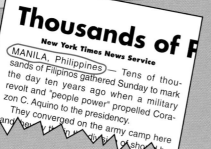

Thousands of F

New York Times News Service

MANILA, Philippines — Tens of thousands of Filipinos gathered Sunday to mark the day ten years ago when a military revolt and "people power" propelled Corazon C. Aquino to the presidency.

They converged on the army camp here

STICKY BUSINESS

- Write a descriptive paragraph about bubble gum. Tell how it looks, smells, feels, tastes, and sounds.
- Think of as many story starters as you can that are about bubble gum. Choose one and write a bubble gum story.
- Count and record how many chews you get from your bubble gum before the taste is gone. Write a letter to Mr. Stick E. Business, of Bubble Power, telling him how to improve the lasting taste of his bubble gum.
- Write down all the ways you can use bubble gum. Be creative!
- Write the directions for blowing a bubble.
- Write a letter to your principal telling him why you think the chewing of bubble gum should be allowed in school.
- List ten reasons why bubble gum cannot be chewed at school on a normal basis. Choose one reason and make a poster to support it.

Sticky Business

Let students stretch their imaginations while having a firsthand experience with bubble gum. List the activities shown on a poster at a center. When a student is ready to visit the center, give him a piece of sugarless bubble gum. Let him chew the gum while he completes his activity at the center; then have him re-wrap the bubble gum and throw it away.

Janice Scott—Gr. 5
Rockport Elementary
Rockport, TX

Chilly Choices

A giant woolen cap can heat up your room with lots of learning! Enlarge the cap pattern on page 99. Color the cap; then mount it on tagboard, laminate it, and cut it out. Each week use a wipe-off marker to list a variety of tasks on the cap. When a student finishes her seatwork, let her choose a task to complete. At the end of the week, wipe the cap clean and reprogram it with new tasks.

List 20 winter words.

Design your own snowflake.

Locate 10 cold cities on a U.S. map.

Write five winter word problems. Solve them.

Illustrate a winter sport.

Write a winter haiku.

Write five synonyms for "cold."

CHILLY CHOICES

- Make a timeline of historic events in sports.
- Design a trophy to represent a particular sport. Write the wording to be engraved on the trophy. Include why and to whom the trophy should be awarded.
- Pretend you are a sports announcer. Write and tape-record a commentary of a famous sports event. Share your recording with the class.
- Write the following categories on a sheet of paper: sports using a ball; sports played inside a building; sports using a stick or racket; sports using a wall, backboard, or net. Write the names of as many sports as you can think of under each category heading.
- Design a badge that might be worn by a fan at your favorite sporting event.
- Pick a star's name from the center and research that person's life history. Write a report that includes your research.
- Design a game involving sports and your favorite sports stars for other students to play. Create the gameboard and playing pieces. Be sure to include directions for play and an answer key if needed.
- Write specific directions to a classmate on how to play a particular sport. Pretend that this person has never seen or played the sport before.

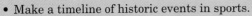

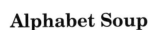

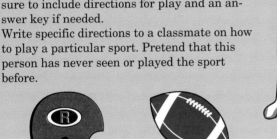

Splendid Sports And Stunning Stars

Students learn about "the thrill of victory and the agony of defeat" in a learning center built around various sports and sports figures. Post magazine and newspaper pictures of athletes in the center. Write the names of various sports on tagboard strips to display with the pictures. Provide star shapes on which each student writes the name of a sports figure and the sport in which that person became famous. Students post the stars in the center.

Write the tasks at the left on index cards decorated with sports-related stickers. Hold the cards together with a pinch clothespin or a metal ring.

Alphabet Soup

For an "mmmmm-good" learning center that provides practice in a variety of skills, serve up a batch of alphabet soup! Duplicate page 100. Have a student volunteer color it and glue it to a sheet of construction paper. Laminate the page; then post it on a bulletin board or at a center for students to work on during free time.

Sr. Jania Keogh—Gr. 4
St. Isidore School
Columbus, NE

Cereal-Box Center

With a snap, crackle, pop, you can make a learning center that's deliciously challenging! Have each student bring an empty cereal box to school. Place the boxes at a center along with a poster listing the tasks below. For an attention-grabbing display, tack some of the boxes on a bulletin board along with the students' work.

Cereal Box Tasks:
- List the different cereals in alphabetical order.
- List each brand of cereal and its price. Why do you think certain cereals cost more than others? Write your answer.
- Choose ten cereals. Estimate the total cost of the cereals; then add to find the actual total.
- Find a cereal box that includes a recipe. Double the recipe.
- Choose five cereals. List them in order according to sugar content.
- Choose one cereal box. Design a new cover for the box.
- Find all of the cereal boxes that offer a free prize inside. Which prize would you most like to have? Give your answer and reasons for your choice in a paragraph.
- Choose one cereal box. Design a simple puzzle that could be printed on the back of the box. Give the puzzle to a friend to solve.
- Choose one cereal box. Write a letter to the president of the cereal company explaining why you do or do not like the box's design.

Deborah Marko—Gr. 4
Price School
Lancaster, PA

Cereal-Box Tasks

- List the different cereals in alphabetical order.
- List each brand of cereal and its price. Why do you think certain cereals cost more than others? Write your answer.
- Choose ten cereals. Estimate the total cost of the cereals; then add to find the actual total.
- Find a cereal box that includes a recipe. Double the recipe.
- Choose fiv_____ order according
- Choose o_____

Pick A Letter

Looking for a free-time activity that's letter-perfect? Look no further! With this fun center, your students will be the proud creators of original books, each one based on a different letter of the alphabet. Duplicate page 101; then have a student color the page and glue it inside a file folder. On the front of the folder, have the student glue colorful alphabet letters cut from various magazines. Give each student a blank folder in which to store his finished book pages. When the books are completed, display them in your school's media center.

Diana Curtis
John Baker Elementary School
Albuquerque, NM

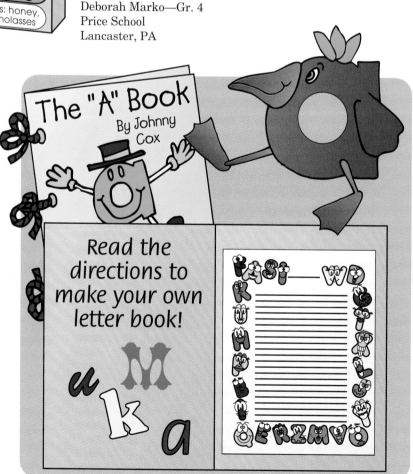

Creatures Of The Past

Even intermediate kids still have a hunger for learning about dinosaurs. To satisfy that hunger and build research skills, make a poster listing activities for each of the following "dino-careers": archaeology, publishing, government, and Creativity, Inc. Provide plenty of dinosaur resources as well as art supplies at a center. Have each student complete one of the tasks from each poster. Or have each child choose a "career." Group kids who choose identical careers in cooperative teams, with each child completing a different activity. However you use these challenging tasks, have students share their efforts on a special "Dino-Day."

Alice N. Rice, Scottsdale, AZ

Archaeology

a. Make a bibliography of dinosaur books in our library.
b. Classify dinosaurs by eating habits, habitat, size, and method of locomotion.
c. Prepare an oral report on animals that are descended from dinosaurs.
d. Write a diary telling about an expedition you went on in your search for dinosaur bones and fossils.

Cre-activity, Inc.

a. Make a model of a dinosaur. Try to use as many unusual materials as you can.
b. Design and draw a new type of dinosaur. Describe its habits on the back of your drawing.
c. List all the possible uses for dinosaurs in the modern world.
d. Design a dinosaur zoo that is an ideal habitat for dinosaurs.

Government

a. Pretend you're a legislator. Write a bill telling what to do about the dinosaurs whose habitat is in the way of a major freeway-building project that citizens have voted to build.
b. Pretend that you are the president. Write a speech recommending whether or not people should be allowed to own dinosaurs as pets.
c. As a judge, you must decide on a fair punishment for a poacher who has been convicted of killing a valuable dinosaur. Write your decision.
d. As an ambassador, you must take a dinosaur to a foreign government as a gift. Write a letter describing what you'll say to the president of this foreign country.

Publishing

a. You've just formed a company to publish a newsletter for dinosaur hobbyists. For your first issue, write a song about how it feels to be a dinosaur.
b. Write a book for young children about a friendly dinosaur and its adventures in the modern world.
c. Pretend that you have a time machine that will take you back to the time of the dinosaurs. Describe what you see and write a story about your adventures.
d. Write an owner's manual for someone who has just bought a dinosaur for a pet.

Spooky Sweet Tooth

A Halloween riddle makes this alphabetizing pocket center appealing. Duplicate page 102. Have a student color the artwork before cutting it out and gluing it to the front of a large manila envelope. Cut out ten large circles from brightly colored paper. Laminate the circles; then use a wipe-off marker to label them with words to alphabetize. For self-checking, program the backs of the cutouts to spell "shockolate" when turned over. Wipe the circles clean to reprogram for sequencing numbers, story events, fractions, or decimals too.

Mr. Jones' Bones

Your students can bone up on math review with this friendly skeleton! Enlarge the skeleton on page 103 on poster board; then laminate it. Use a wipe-off marker to label the skeleton's bones with math problems as shown. Display the skeleton at a center equipped with multiple copies of the worksheet on page 103. A student visiting the center solves the problems on the giant skeleton and writes his answers on a copy of the worksheet, making sure that he places each answer on the corresponding bone. To use the skeleton again, simply wipe it clean and reprogram with new problems.

Donna Frazier
Woodville, AL

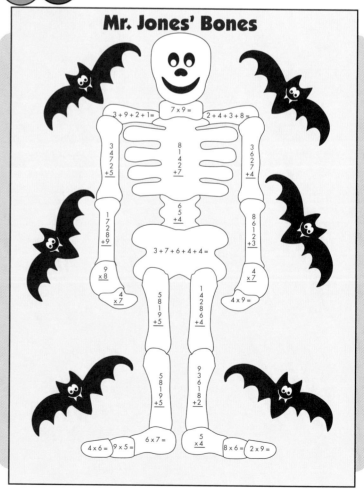

Personal Pumpkins

Every student needs practice reading and following directions. Clip a tagboard pumpkin pattern as shown inside the folder. Post the personalized pumpkins on your wall or door.

Sandra Steen—Gr. 4
Corinth, MS

Steps:
1. Get a pencil, black crayon, scissors, and an orange piece of paper.
2. Use a pencil to trace the pattern onto the orange paper. Be sure to draw the mouth as shown on the pattern.
3. Use a pencil to write your name in capital letters inside the mouth. Stretch the letters to fill up the mouth.
4. Use a pencil to add a stem, a nose, and two eyes.
5. Go over your pencil lines with black crayon.
6. Cut out the pumpkin.

Follow the directions to make your own Halloween pumpkin.

Pattern

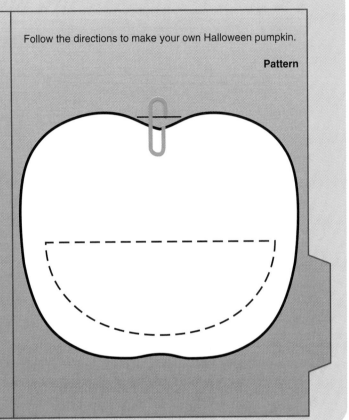

The Most Ghosts

Practice math skills with a "spooktacular" center. Duplicate page 104. Have a student color the page (leaving the windows uncolored) and glue it to a sheet of construction paper. Laminate the center; then use a wipe-off marker to program each window with a math problem. Place an answer key in a pocket attached to the back of the center. To change the skill, simply wipe the windows clean and reprogram.

Puzzling Package

Celebrate the holiday of Hanukkah with this fun folder. To make the activity even more appealing, cut the folder in the shape of a holiday package. Write the answer key on an index card and glue it to the back of the folder.

Hanukkah is a Jewish holiday in December. It is also called the Festival of Lights. Use letters in "Festival of Lights" to make a word for each definition. Write the words on your paper. Use the key to check.

1. What a thief does (5 letters)
2. What you study for (4 letters)
3. A sleeveless jacket (4 letters)
4. What a boxer does (6 letters)
5. Opposite of "take" (4 letters)
6. 50 percent (4 letters)
7. Opposite of "big" (6 letters)
8. A small cut (4 letters)
9. Sick (3 letters)
10. What you stand on (4 letters)
11. Opposite of "cold" (3 letters)
12. Opposite of "fresh" (5 letters)

Now, make up three more puzzles using the letters. Give them to a friend to solve!

Answer Key
1. steal
2. test
3. vest
4. fights
5. give
6. half
7. little
8. slit
9. ill
10. legs
11. hot
12. stale

December Writing Cards

Preparing a December writing center is a snap with the reproducible activity cards found on pages 105–108. Duplicate the pages; then glue them to construction paper. Laminate the cards and cut them apart. Place the cards in a holiday cookie tin, gift box, or stocking. Or store the cards in a file folder decorated with pictures students have cut from holiday greeting cards.

To help students keep track of their writing, provide a supply of holiday gift tags. Give each child a blank file folder. Have the student store his work in the folder. Each time a student completes one of the activities, have him write the number of the card on a gift tag and glue it inside his folder. Initial the tag after you have reviewed the student's work.

29. Santa's tired of cookies and milk on Christmas Eve. List ten snacks that Santa has probably never had on Christmas Eve.

3. Write an ad for the Yellow Pages describing a store that sells toys which are guaranteed not to break.

TOYS!

Magnificent Mini-Folders

This Christmas, pack your writing center with handy mini-folders. Cut regular file folders in half. Glue an illustration from a Christmas card to the front of each mini-folder. Write a story starter inside. For personification practice, have children write stories describing Christmas from the point of view of some unusual holiday objects.

Story Starters: What would Christmas be like if you were:

1. A gift tag on a package for the President?
2. Steve Urkel's Christmas tree?
3. Deion Sanders's Santa Claus suit?
4. The Queen of England's Christmas stocking?
5. David Letterman's potted poinsettia?
6. Michael Bolton's favorite Christmas album?
7. Whitney Houston's Christmas wreath?
8. Michael Jordan's last roll of Christmas wrapping paper?

What could Christmas be like if you were:

Michael Jordan's last roll of Christmas wrapping paper?

2.

Bill Cosby (1937–) is a comedian and was the star of his own program, "The Cosby Show." He costarred in the mid-'60s in the action series "I Spy." He also created and hosted the "Fat Albert and the Cosby Kids" cartoon. Cosby has sold more comedy records than anyone in the world. He's also the author of several popular books.

12.

Coretta Scott King (1927–) works for the civil rights of blacks and other minorities. She is the widow of Dr. Martin Luther King, Jr. While her husband was working to win more rights for black Americans, Mrs. King gave speeches and lectures. After Dr. King was killed, Mrs. King continued working for civil rights.

To Do: What rights do you think all Americans should enjoy? Make a list of at least ten of these rights.

Afro-American History Month Activity Cards

Celebrate Afro-American History Month with the reproducible activity cards featured on pages 109–112. Duplicate the cards; then mount them on construction paper and laminate them. Cut the cards apart and store them in a box. Or punch a hole in the corner of each card and store on a metal ring. Display your students' finished work from the cards on a bulletin board entitled "They Believed. They Achieved!" Encourage further research by adding this list of other famous African Americans to the display:

Duke Ellington
Marian Anderson
Jesse Owens
Roy Wilkins
Richard Wright
Benjamin Banneker
Richmond Barthé
Henry O. Tanner
Ralph J. Bunche
Maggie M. Walker

Katherine Dunham
W.E.B. Du Bois
Joe Louis
Lewis H. Latimer
Crispus Attucks
Malcolm X
Phillis Wheatley
Wilma Rudolph
Bill Russell

Talking With George And Abe

Introduce students to George Washington and Abraham Lincoln through creative writing. Write these tasks on index cards and place them at a center with resource books, cartridge pens, and paper. Students choose one task and use pen and ink to make authentic-looking, aged documents.

- Imagine you are a talk-show host. Write a conversation between George and Abe that occurred on your show. What questions did George ask Abe about the Civil War? What were Abe's answers?
- Who was the better president: Abe or George? Defend your view. Give at least three sentences to support your opinion.
- Write some advice that George might have given Abe if he had been alive when Abe was president.
- Design and describe a new memorial or monument to the memory of these two beloved men.
- Design a stamp honoring one of these great presidents. Tell what the stamp commemorates.

Mary Anne T. Haffner
Waynesboro, PA

Mail Call

Use inexpensive valentines to make grammar practice a treat. Attach three construction-paper mailbags to the inside of a folder for pockets. Circle one word on each of 20 valentines. Students look at the circled word on each valentine and place it in the correct pocket. Code the backs of the valentines for self-checking.

Place each valentine in the correct mailbag. Look on the back of each valentine to check.

NOUN

VERB

ADJECTIVE

You are tops in every "cat-egory"!

Swimmin' Through Spring

Looking for the perfect bait to lure your students into springtime skill practice? Make this simple learning center display with the help of your kids and pages 56 and 81.

with contributions by Laurie Vent, Upper Sandusky, OH

List five ways that you are like and five ways that you are unlike a kite.

How Do I Set Up The Display?

It's easy! Just cover a bulletin board or door with blue background paper. Staple a strip of tan paper along the bottom of the board to make the ocean floor. Add the title "Swimmin' Through Spring." Next duplicate the fish patterns (page 81) on white construction paper. With a permanent marker, number and label each fish with one of the tasks listed on page 56.

How Can I Involve My Students?

Have students color the labeled fish and cut them out. After stapling the fish to the board, let students add construction paper shells, plants, sea creatures—even a treasure chest!

How Do I Manage The Display And My Students?

You may wish to require each student to complete a designated number of tasks while the display is up. Or you may want to use the tasks for extra credit or free-time work.

How Do I Evaluate Student Work?

Rather than giving letter grades, tell students that they will help each other determine whether work is "Satisfactory" or "Needs More Work." Divide students into work teams. Set aside time for brief team meetings every few days. At the meetings, team members evaluate each other's work and determine whether it is ready to turn in. Be sure to mount student work around the display.

How Can I Adapt This Display?

Program the fish with math problems, spelling words to unscramble, vocabulary words to define, or titles of good books to read. For a motivational display, change the title to "Nothing Fishy About This Class!" Add a cut-out fish to the board each day students exhibit a desired behavior. When a predetermined number of fish are on the board, treat the class to a favorite video and a snack of goldfish crackers!

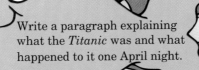

Mother Goose Day is May 1. Rewrite a nursery rhyme as a rap song.

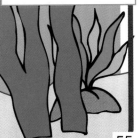

Write a paragraph explaining what the *Titanic* was and what happened to it one April night.

Activities For "Swimmin' Through Spring" on page 55.

1. April is Keep America Beautiful Month. Draw a picture showing at least three things that you think make America beautiful.

2. Earth Day is April 22. List ways our school can save energy or recycle materials.

3. Reading Is Fun Week is in April. Read a FUNny story. Draw a picture of the funniest part.

4. May is American Bike Month. Use an encyclopedia to list five ways that today's bikes are different from the first bikes.

5. The first postage stamp was issued on May 6, 1840. Design a stamp to honor the person you admire most.

6. Write a letter to your mom (or other relative) describing your favorite memory of the two of you together.

7. National Library Week is in April. Design a billboard to encourage people to visit the library.

8. April is National Humor Month. Write a paragraph advising someone who wants to make you laugh.

9. List five ways that you are like and five ways that you are unlike a kite.

10. Write a paragraph explaining what the *Titanic* was and what happened to it one April night.

11. List at least seven ways that you would celebrate Thanksgiving if it were suddenly moved to May.

12. Law Day is May 1. Do you think this world needs more laws or fewer laws? Explain your answer.

13. Mother Goose Day is May 1. Rewrite a nursery rhyme as a rap song.

14. National Pet Week is in May. Draw or describe the perfect pet for your favorite entertainer.

15. Find a poem about spring. Write a paragraph giving reasons why you do or do not like the poem.

Positive Messages

Help students focus on the positive points of their classmates with this center activity. After each student makes a booklet, pass them out. Have students write positive messages inside the books about their owners. Collect the books and repeat this procedure until every student has written in each book. After several weeks each child will receive a book full of positive messages about himself. Be sure to make a book yourself and participate in the writings.

Center supplies:

9" x 12" construction paper in assorted colors
8 1/2" x 11" white paper
stapler
crayons or markers

Mary Anne Haffner
Waynesboro, PA

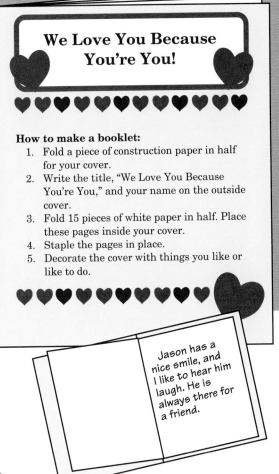

We Love You Because You're You!

How to make a booklet:

1. Fold a piece of construction paper in half for your cover.
2. Write the title, "We Love You Because You're You," and your name on the outside cover.
3. Fold 15 pieces of white paper in half. Place these pages inside your cover.
4. Staple the pages in place.
5. Decorate the cover with things you like or like to do.

Jason has a nice smile, and I like to hear him laugh. He is always there for a friend.

Circle every mistake on the worksheet.

Authorized Undercover Assignment

This "Undercover Center" challenges secret agents to find mistakes. Each week I place copies of a worksheet containing numerous mistakes in a special laminated "Undercover Center" folder. I leave one clue (written on the front of the folder with a wipe-off marker): the total number of mistakes on the page. Students circle and tally incorrect items. It's a fun way to help students read for detail and reinforce previously taught skills. Present awards or coupons to successful secret agents.

Sr. Margaret Ann Wooden
Martinsburg, WV

You Oughta Be In Pictures!

Inexpensive photo albums—the ones that hold one photo per page—can be turned into instant learning centers. I cut out pictures of animals from magazines and place them in one album. On the opposite side of each picture, I list the animal's name. I've also created albums that reinforce math vocabulary, geometric terms and definitions, and story problems. Students solve the problem or answer the question on a right-hand page; then they turn the page to check the answer. These photo-album centers are easy to make, and students love to use them!

Carol Stanfill
Pagosa Elementary
Pagosa Springs, CO

anteater

a parallelogram with four equal sides and sometimes one with no right angles

polygon

FIND YOUR CLASSMATES

Choose a name search puzzle. Cover it with an acetate sheet. Then use a wipe-off marker to circle as many of your classmates' names as possible.

T	I	F	F	A	N	Y	X
A	T	N	E	C	N	I	O
M	I	C	H	A	E	L	K
M	Z	N	M	K	R	R	E
Y	A	C	E	J	I	M	L
T	C	J	O	H	N	J	L
S	H	E	I	L	A	N	I
W	E	N	D	Y	D	O	E

Jim	Tammy	Sheila
John	Tiffany	Wendy
Michael	Erin	Kellie
Juan	Amin	Tia
Kelly	Marcus	Min

Find Your Classmates

At the beginning of the year, have students get acquainted with this fun center idea. Give each child a duplicated grid and class list. Have each student try to hide as many of his classmates' names as possible in his grid. Mount a poster as shown at a learning center. Place the completed name search puzzles at the center, along with a supply of wipe-off markers and acetate sheets.

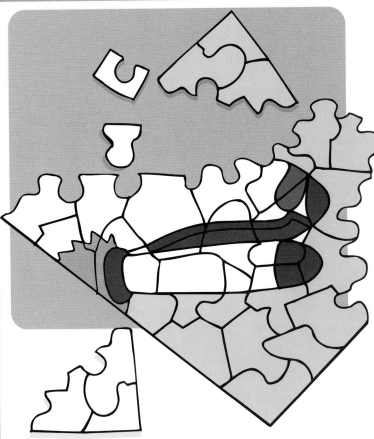

Puzzle Power

For an easy-to-manage free-time activity, I keep a large jigsaw puzzle on a corner table. The puzzle usually relates to a current science or social studies topic. A student may work on the puzzle after she has completed all of her assignments. To make sure that no more than four students work on the puzzle at a time, I post a sign-up sheet nearby.

When a puzzle is completed, we preserve it with puzzle glue (available at craft stores). Each student who worked on the puzzle writes her name on a slip of paper and places it in a jar. I draw one name from the jar and present the puzzle to that lucky student.

Marsha Goode—Gr. 5
Creekview School
Middletown, OH

Changeable Cardboard Centers

All you need to create a supply of easy-to-adapt, thematic centers is a cardboard box. Cut the sides of the box apart so that you have four to six square or rectangular pieces. Cut a piece of construction paper to cover one side of each piece of cardboard. Laminate these pieces of construction paper before mounting them on the cardboard.

On each piece of construction paper, use rubber cement to mount pictures and task cards relating to a particular theme, such as whales. Place the centers on a chalk tray, clip them on a clothesline, or store them in a box. The rubber cement will hold the pieces firmly in place, but peels right off when you're ready to change the pictures and task cards.

Stationery Center

For a learning center that's long on usability and short on preparation time, try this earth-friendly idea. Save all of your old greeting cards, wrapping paper scraps, wallpaper samples, buttons, stamps, and other recyclable materials. Place them in colorful folders or inexpensive plastic baskets at a center equipped with glue, scissors, construction paper, and other art supplies. Students visiting the center use the materials to make original greeting cards, notepads, or writing paper for themselves or to give as gifts. Replenish your center with donations from students, co-workers, and friends.

Carrie Cruthers—Gr. 4 Teacher's Aide
Willo-Hill Christian School, Willoughby, OH

Centers-To-Go

I've collected a supply of small fruit baskets with handles. Inside the baskets, I place such items as memo pads, pencils, small writing tablets, crayons, large erasers, photographs, and index cards labeled with story starters. The baskets take up very little storage space and can be moved to any area in the room to be used. I fill other baskets with center activities for math, science, literature, and social studies. These centers-to-go are great for an absent student who has missed critical lessons. I can fill a basket with center activities that will help the student to catch up in no time. The child can even take the basket home and return it the following day.

Denise Mills— Gr. 4
Livingston Elementary
Covington, GA

ABRACADABRA— Two Centers In One!

If you've got a classroom table, you've got two centers in one! I place all needed materials for my math or science center on top of a table. To make a second center without using additional space, I tape posters under the tabletop. Each poster is labeled with math problems to solve, story starters, or other tasks. Along a nearby wall, I've attached paper pockets to hold all of the necessary materials for completing the posters' tasks. My students love to recline under the table on mats and complete the activities.

Denise Mills—Gr. 4
Livingston Elementary
Covington, GA

Centers On A Line

If you've got a clothesline in your classroom, you've got a handy tool for storing centers. Fold several large pieces of poster board as shown; then staple the sides of each to make a large pocket. (I decorate each pocket by covering it with wallpaper samples.) Inside each pocket, insert games, writing ideas, task cards, and other center activities. Use pinch clothespins to clip the center pockets on a clothesline that's been strung along a wall, below the chalkboard tray, or at the back of the room. A student selects a pocket, unclips it from the line, and returns to his desk to complete the activity inside. Make the pockets self-checking by inserting answer keys.

Denise Mills—Gr. 4
Livingston Elementary
Covington, GA

Pattern

Use with "Hang In There!" on page 4.

Hang In There!

Write the following categories on your paper: nouns, verbs, adverbs, adjectives. Place each of the words in one or more of the categories. Check your work with a dictionary.

Create a "memory sentence" for each word on the list to help you better remember its spelling. A classic example that stands for *arithmetic* is: "A rat in the house might eat the ice cream."

Boost your dictionary skills. Write down the root, origin, and one definition of each of the words.

Work with a partner. One person calls out a word to the other. The partner spells the word frontwards and then backwards. See how many each player spells correctly.

Use the beginning sound of each word to write an alliterative sentence. For example:
CAT = Crazy Calvin called Clara a "cool cat."

1. _____

2. _____

3. _____

4. _____

5. _____

6. _____

7. _____

8. _____

9. _____

10. _____

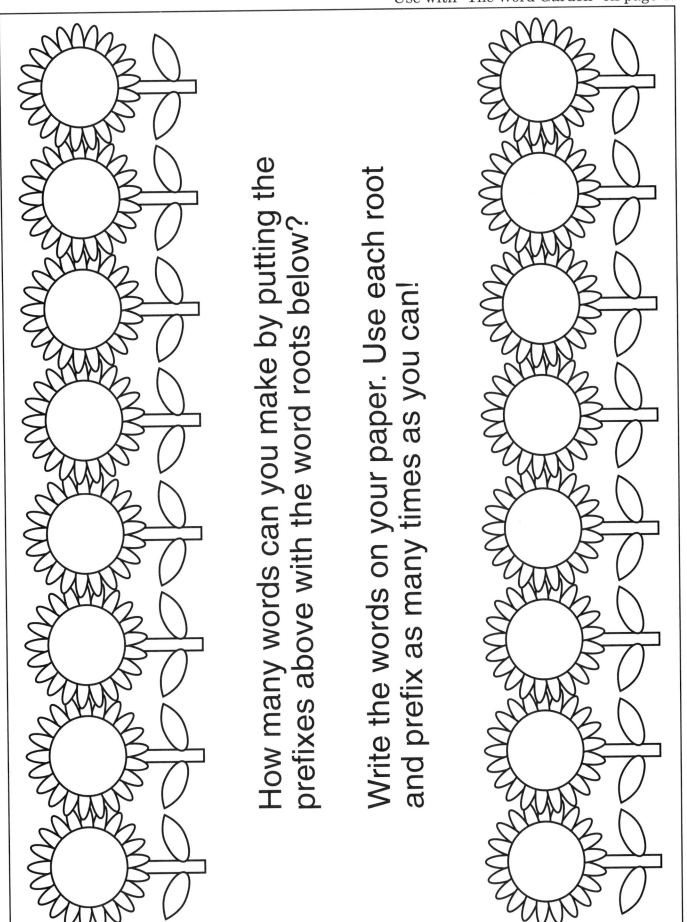

How many words can you make by putting the prefixes above with the word roots below?

Write the words on your paper. Use each root and prefix as many times as you can!

Pattern

Use with "Adjective And Noun Ding-a-lings" on page 5.

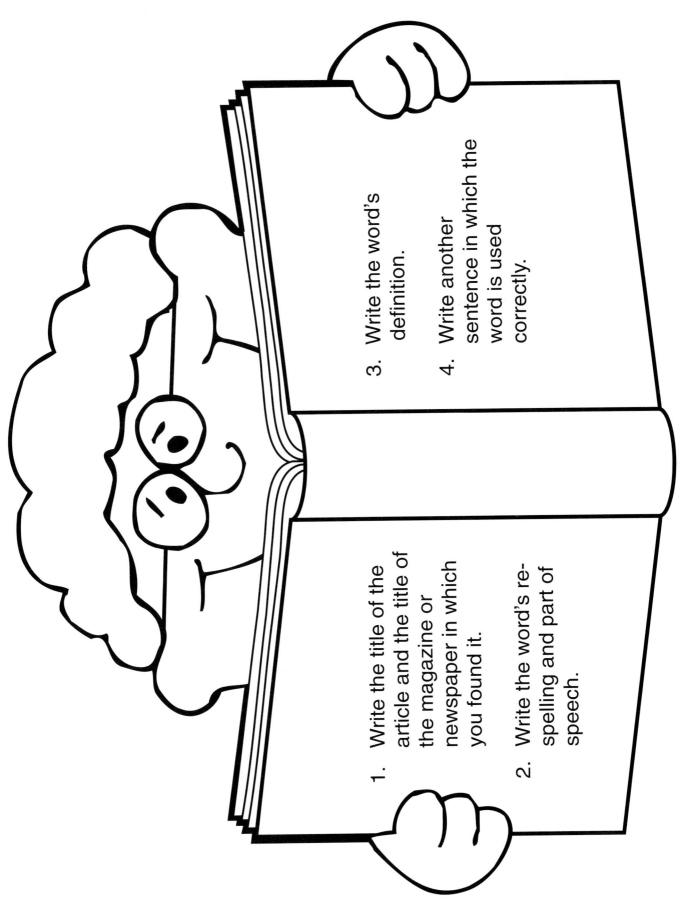

1. Write the title of the article and the title of the magazine or newspaper in which you found it.

2. Write the word's re-spelling and part of speech.

3. Write the word's definition.

4. Write another sentence in which the word is used correctly.

Patterns

Use with "Catch Feline Fever" on page 6.

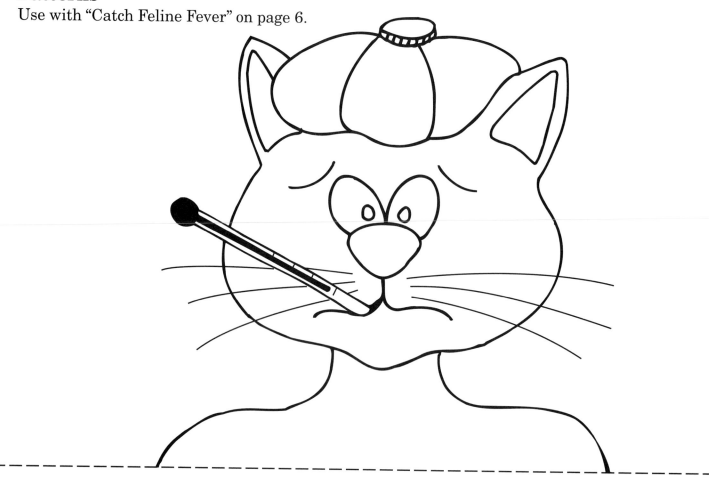

1. What cat is an ancient military weapon used to hurl missiles?
2. What cat changes to a butterfly?
3. What cat is a tree?
4. What cat lists things for sale?
5. What cats are ranch animals?
6. What cat is a hamburger condiment?
7. What cat is a waterfall or a clouding of the lens of the eye?
8. What cat stands behind home plate?
9. What cat is a plant cats love?
10. What cat is big trouble?
11. What cats grow in marshes?
12. What cat is an ancient burial place?
13. What cat is an earthquake?
14. What cat is a class or division?

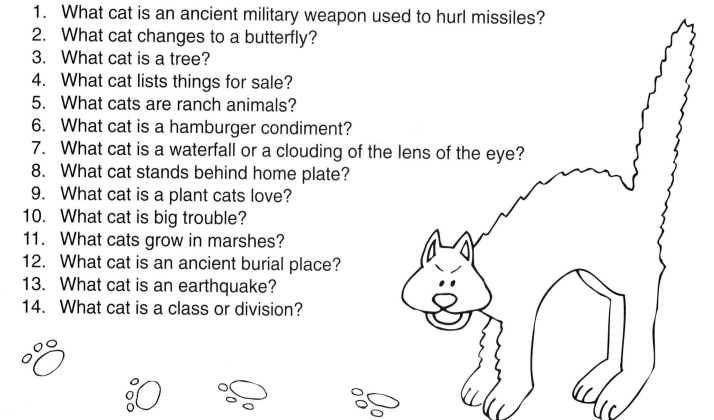

Who Did It?

1. "Jane and me went shopping that morning," said Mona.
2. Jane and Mona is in real trouble.
3. Jane gave the candlestick to her father as a gift.
4. Sidney likes to play tennis.
5. Does Jane and Sidney play tennis together?
6. Sam found a tennis racket beside the ransom note.
7. A pillow lay on the floor beside Marvin's bed.
8. A book lied open on the table.
9. Suzanne said, "Hand me one of them books."
10. "Sit the book on the table there," said Sam.
11. Suzanne has really growed up.
12. Jake didn't never like Marvin.

Jane, the wife 56

Sam, the butler 55

Mona, the sister-in-law 40

Sidney, the business partner 48

Suzanne, the maid 58

Jake, the father-in-law 46

Pattern
Use with "Word Web" on page 9.

past

present

future

speak

invent

throw

draw

drive

forget

bring

catch

spin

write

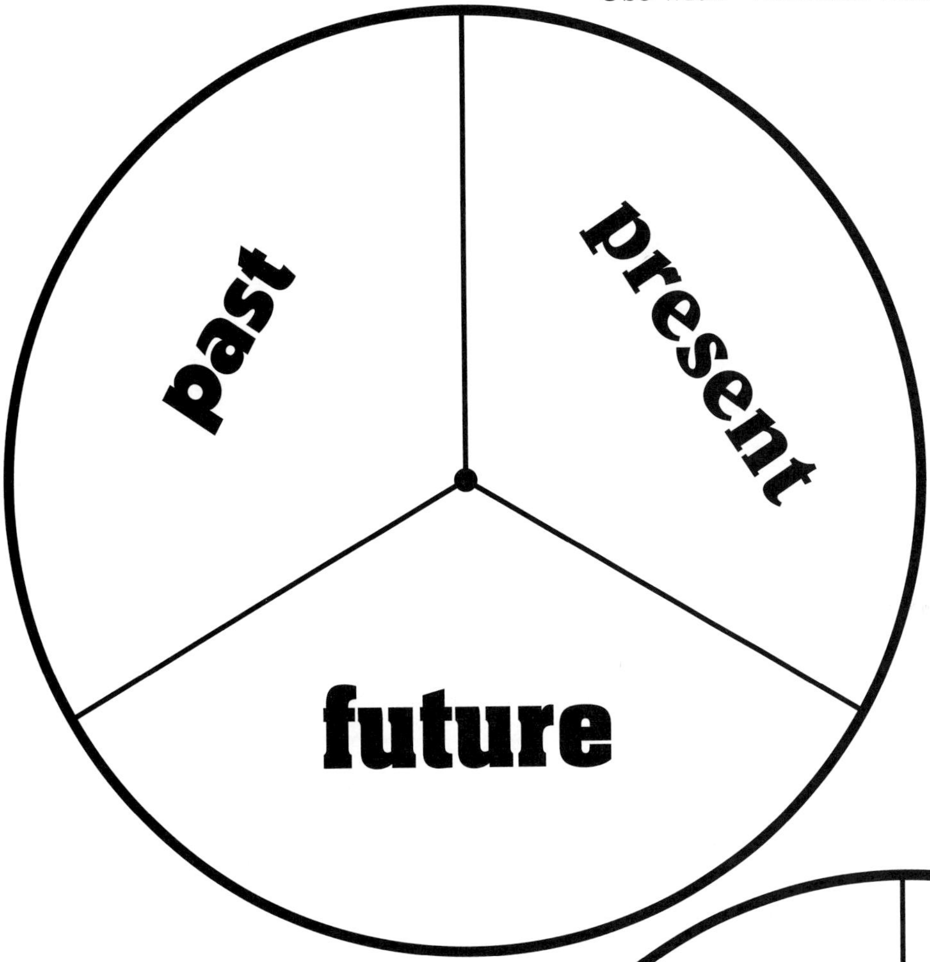

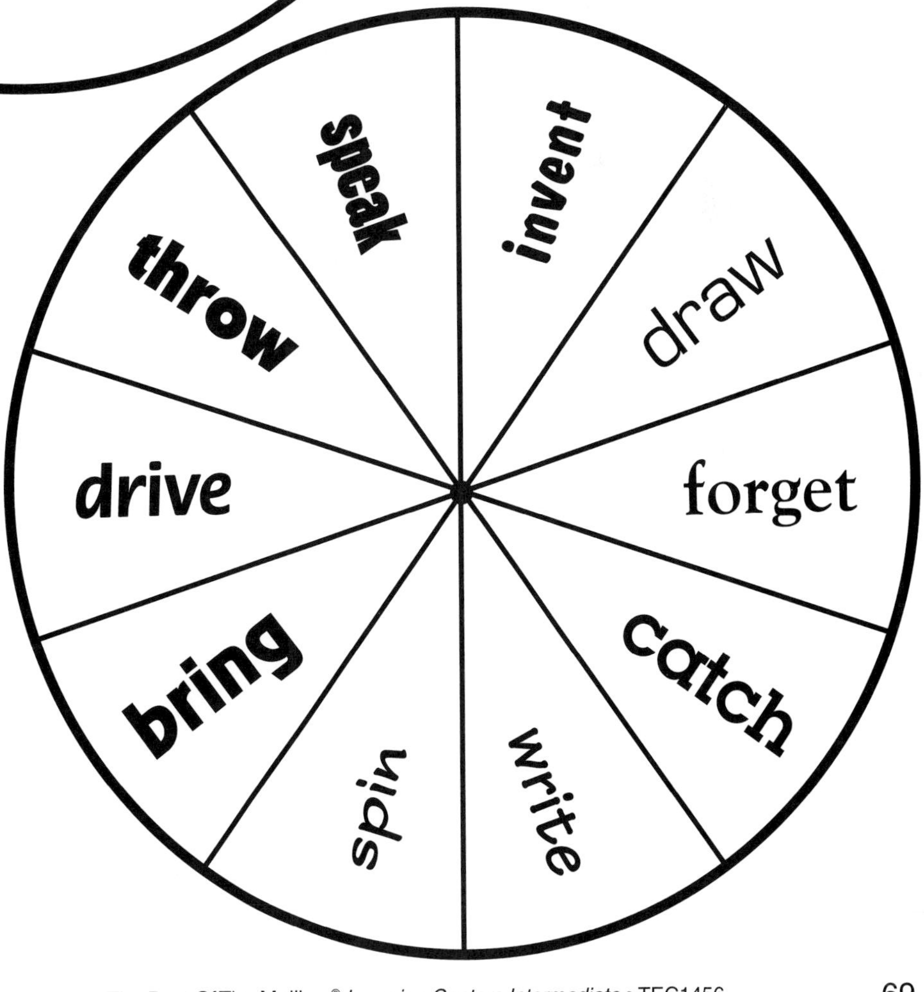

Pattern
Use with "Idiomagic!" on page 11.

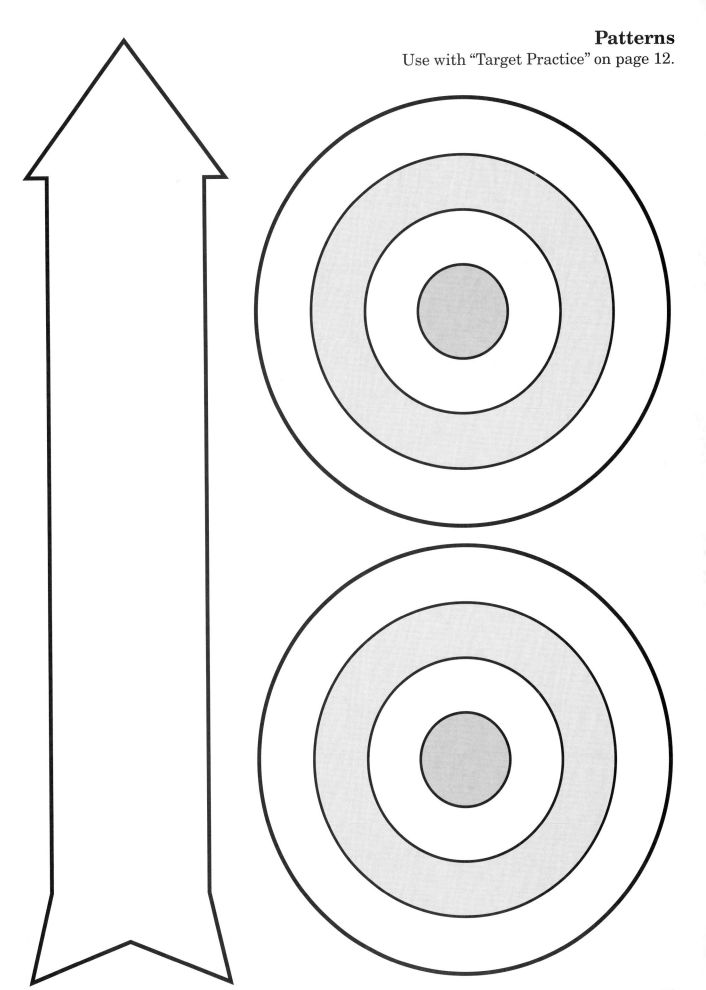

Pattern

Use with "Fishy Facts" on page 14.

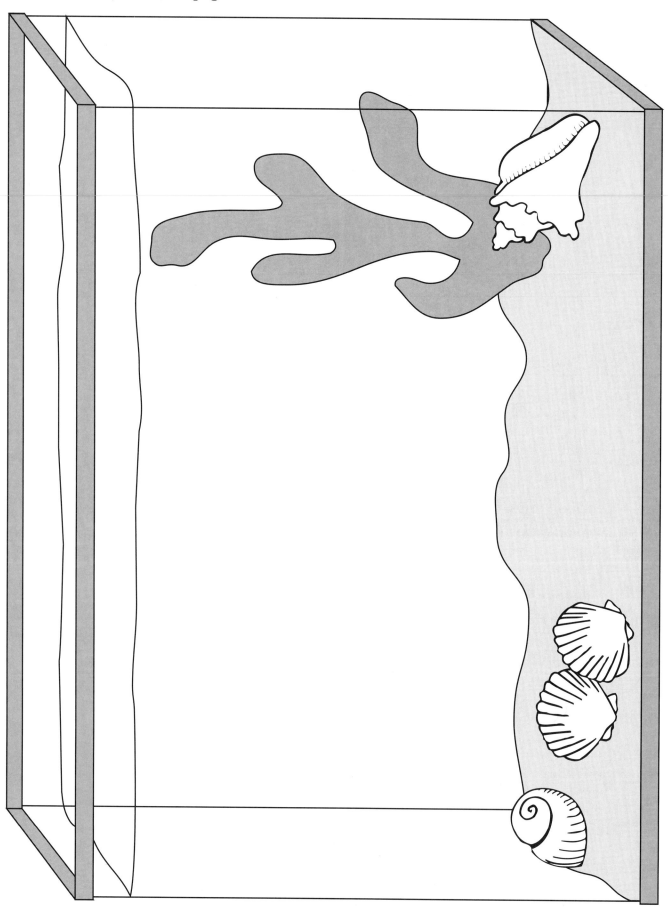

Patterns

Use with "Bananas About Books!" on page 14.

Activity #1
Write about the most exciting part of this story. Or write about the most boring part.

On My Honor

Activity #2
Describe the setting of this story (where and when it took place). Draw a picture of the setting.

The Great Brain

Activity #3
Draw a picture of your favorite part of this story. Add a caption explaining what is happening in your picture.

The Pinballs

Activity #4
Make a time line showing the important events of this story. Draw some pictures on your time line, too.

Dear Mr. Henshaw

Activity #5
What do you think are the five most important events in this story? List them in order of importance, beginning with the most important event.

The Hundred Dresses

Activity #6
Choose one character in this story. Think about what that character was like at the beginning of the story. Write about how the character had changed by the end of the story.

The Slave Dancer

Activity #7
If you could trade places with any character in this story, who would you choose? Write about why you chose this character.

The Cay

Activity #8
Which character in this story is most unlike you? Write about how you are different from this character. Tell whether you think you and this character could be good friends.

The Night Swimmers

Patterns

Use with "Bananas About Books!" on page 14.

Activity #9

Write an *ode* to this story. (An ode is a type of poem that doesn't have to rhyme.)

Caddie Woodlaw

Activity #10

Pretend that you have been chosen to write a sequel to this story. Write a brief summary of the sequel. Include information about the sequel's *plot, setting,* and *main characters.*

Harriet The Spy

Activity #11

Make a bookmark illustrating this story. On the back of the bookmark, write at least five words you would use to describe this story.

Soup

Activity #12

Make a word search, crossword, or other puzzle using at least ten new vocbulary words from this story. Make an answer key. Give your puzzle to a friend to solve.

SOUNDER

Activity #13
What award would you nominate this story for? Most Exciting? Most Likely To Make You Laugh Your Head Off? Write about the award you would give to this story. Tell why you chose this award.

Blubber

Activity #14
Write about the pages you read today.

The Westing Game

Activity #15
Think about the setting of this story. Write about why you would or would not like to spend a week visiting this place.

The Enormous Egg

Activity #16
Write about one problem in this story and how the character(s) solved it. Was it a good solution? Why or why not?

OLD YELLER

Pattern
Use with "The Olde Curiosity Shoppe" on page 15.

The Olde Curiosity Shoppe

©1996 The Education Center, Inc. • *The Best Of* The Mailbox® *Learning Centers Intermediate* • TEC1456

Use with "Guide-Word Guides" on page 16.

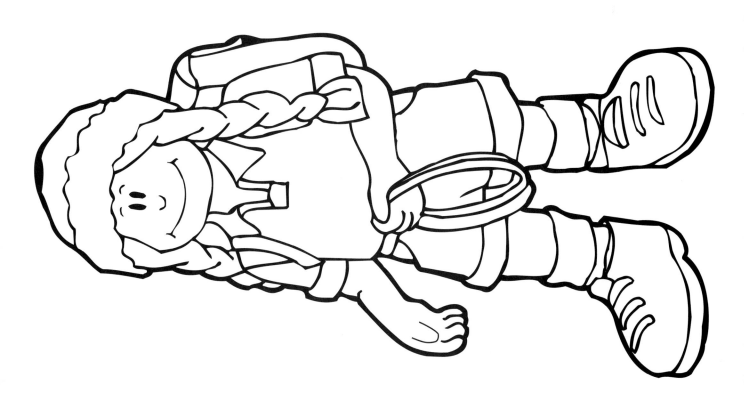

Pattern

Use with "Guide-Word Guides" on page 16.

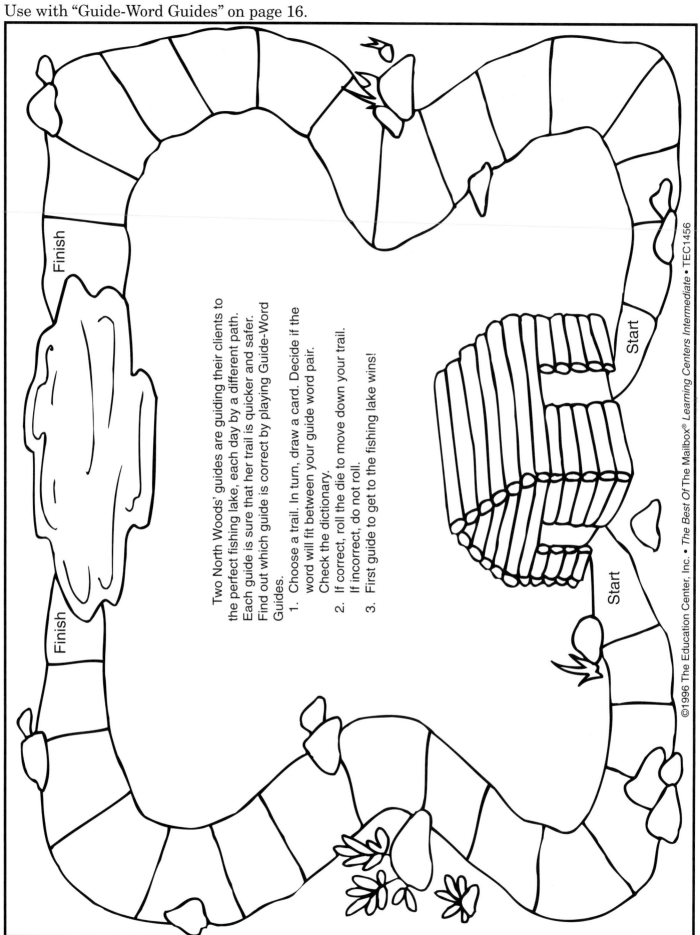

Finish

Finish

Start

Start

Two North Woods' guides are guiding their clients to the perfect fishing lake, each day by a different path. Each guide is sure that her trail is quicker and safer. Find out which guide is correct by playing Guide-Word Guides.

1. Choose a trail. In turn, draw a card. Decide if the word will fit between your guide word pair. Check the dictionary.

2. If correct, roll the die to move down your trail. If incorrect, do not roll.

3. First guide to get to the fishing lake wins!

Pattern

Use with "Believe It Or Not!" on page 21.

R.I.P.

Pattern
Use with "Mail Call!" on page 27.

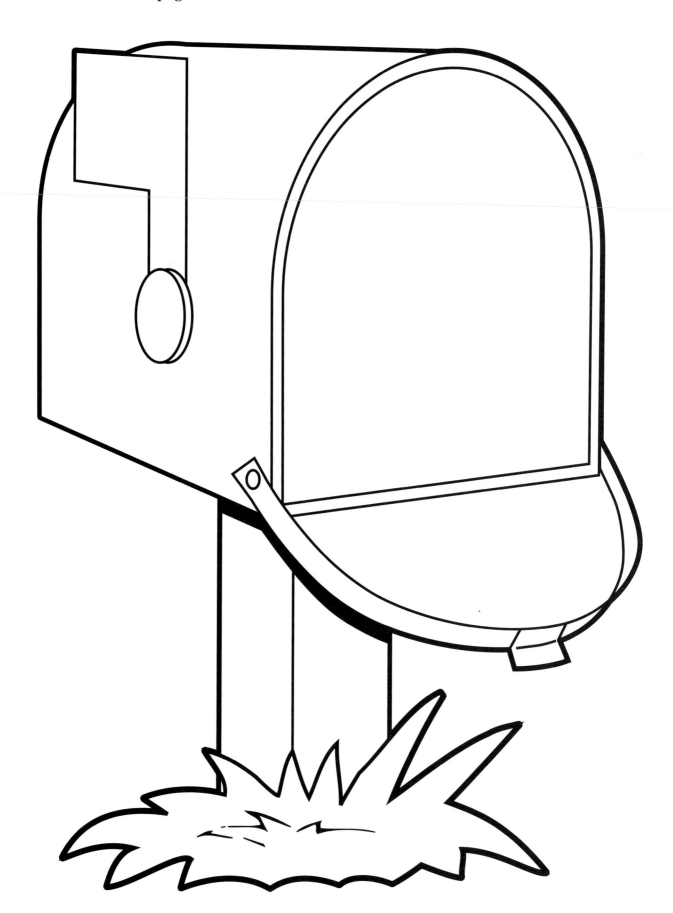

Use with "Magical Mythmakers" on page 31.

SITTING PRETTY

Spin the spinner; then write and solve each math problem on your paper. Have a partner check your work.

Surf's Up!

Sweet Treats

On your paper, write the place value of each underlined digit.

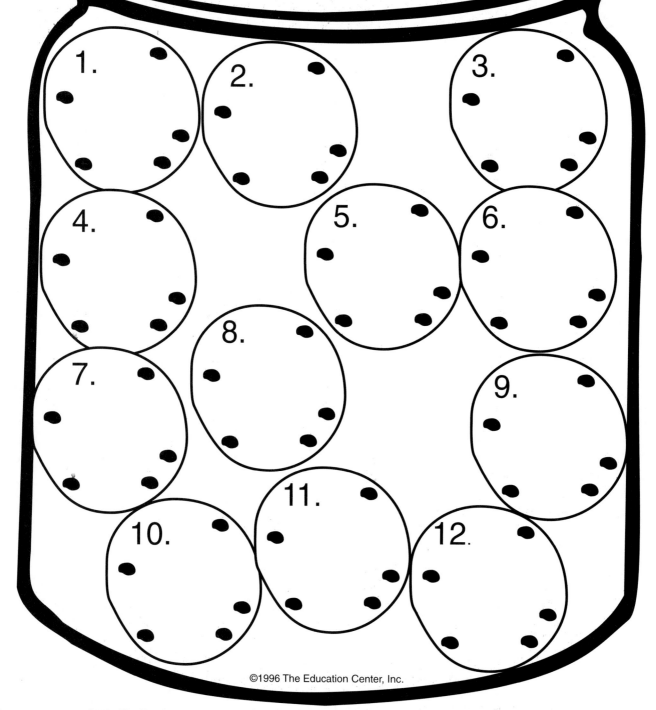

1.
2.
3.
4.
5.
6.
7.
8.
9.
10.
11.
12.

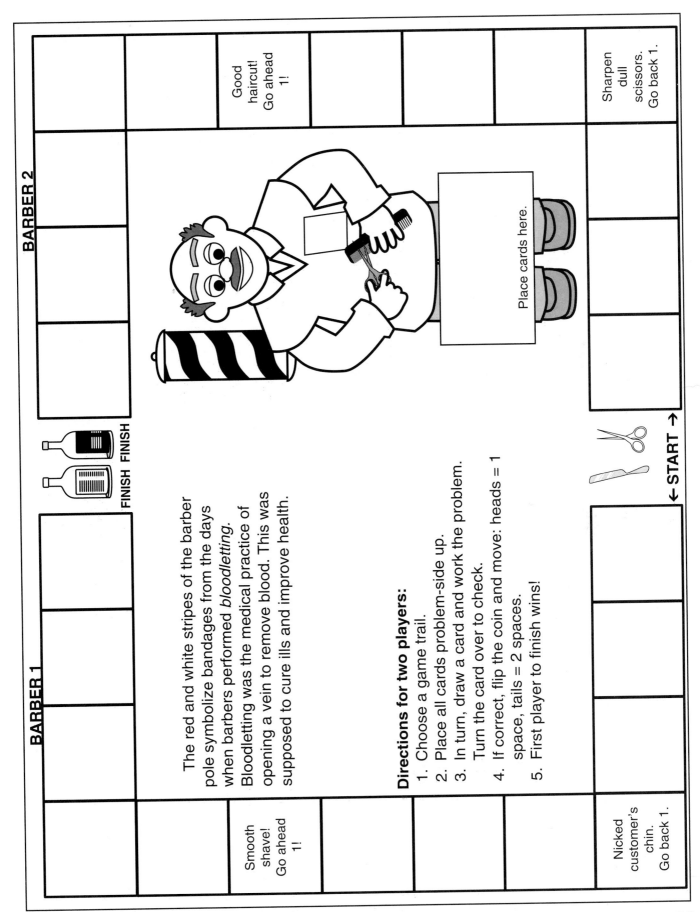

BARBER 2

BARBER 1

Good haircut! Go ahead 1!

Sharpen dull scissors. Go back 1.

FINISH FINISH

Place cards here.

← START →

The red and white stripes of the barber pole symbolize bandages from the days when barbers performed *bloodletting*. Bloodletting was the medical practice of opening a vein to remove blood. This was supposed to cure ills and improve health.

Directions for two players:
1. Choose a game trail.
2. Place all cards problem-side up.
3. In turn, draw a card and work the problem. Turn the card over to check.
4. If correct, flip the coin and move: heads = 1 space, tails = 2 spaces.
5. First player to finish wins!

Smooth shave! Go ahead 1!

Nicked customer's chin. Go back 1.

Patterns

Use with "How Do You Eat Your Jumly?" on page 38.

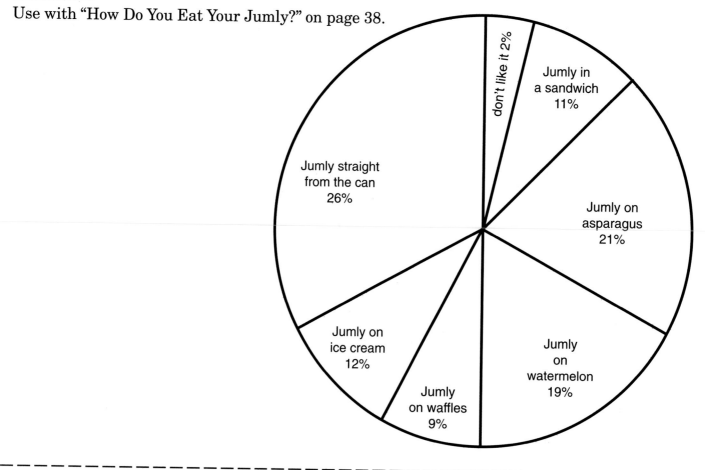

Circle graph showing: don't like it 2%; Jumly in a sandwich 11%; Jumly straight from the can 26%; Jumly on asparagus 21%; Jumly on ice cream 12%; Jumly on waffles 9%; Jumly on watermelon 19%

- -

Nosy Rosy did a survey for the makers of Jumly, a brand-new food. She asked 200 people, "How do you eat your Jumly?" She showed the results on a circle graph. Use the information from the graph to answer these questions on your paper.

1. What percentage of people eat Jumly in a sandwich?
2. How do most people surveyed eat their Jumly?
3. Do more people eat Jumly on asparagus or on waffles?
4. What percentage of people eat Jumly either on watermelon or ice cream?
5. What percentage of people eat Jumly either on waffles or from the can?

The whole graph represents the total number of people interviewed—200 people or 100%. To find out how many people like Jumly straight from the can, multiply 200 by 26%.

26% x 200 = 0.26 x 200 = 52 people like Jumly from the can

How many people like:

6. Jumly in a sandwich?
7. Jumly on ice cream?
8. Jumly on watermelon?

Patterns

Use with "Shady Business" on page 41.

Name _____

Estimation

Estimate the weight of each item in your sandwich bag and record your prediction below. Weigh each item using the scale and the paper clips. Record your findings. Finally, subtract to find the difference between each estimation and actual weight.

Remember: one small paper clip weighs approximately one gram.

GRAMS

	Estimated Weight	Actual Weight	Difference
peanut	_____	_____	_____
marshmallow	_____	_____	_____
jelly bean	_____	_____	_____
Mini Oreo®	_____	_____	_____
Gummy Bear®	_____	_____	_____
Skittle®	_____	_____	_____

1. dwarf: giant   as   small: L A R G E
2. palm: coconut   as   oak: _ _ _ _ _
3. mountain: altitude   as   ocean: _ _ _ _ _
4. fawn: doe   as   child: _ _ _ _ _ _
5. captain: ship   as   pilot: _ _ _ _ _ _
6. fruit: orchard   as   fish: _ _ _ _ _
7. hand: arm   as   foot: _ _ _
8. sneaker: shoe   as   watch: _ _ _ _ _
9. hair: barber   as   teeth: _ _ _ _ _ _
10. hot: cold   as   beginning: _ _ _ _

Now, write the first letter of each word you wrote in the numbered blanks below to find out what the sneezing champion of the Olympics wins.

_ _ _ <u>L</u> _   _ _ _ _ _
2   8 6 1 9   4 10 3 5 7

Pattern

Use with "Think Or Sink!" on page 43.

THINK OR SINK!

Put on your thinking cap! Choose a question to answer. Write and illustrate your answer.

1. If you could add one day to every week, what would you name that day? Why would you choose that name?
2. What animal would make the greatest best friend? Explain your answer.
3. Besides brushing your teeth, what else can a toothbrush be used for?
4. List some words that make beautiful sounds.
5. Think of five uses for an old sneaker.
6. What do you suppose the president of the United States wore on Halloween when he was a kid?
7. What is the most useless thing in your bedroom right now? Explain your answer.
8. Design a way to wash dishes while lying down (no dishwasher allowed).
9. If you could read the mind of anyone in the world, whose mind would you choose and why?
10. Describe a recent meal without including the names of any foods or drinks.
11. You are interviewing your hero but can ask him or her only five questions. What questions would you ask?
12. Describe an event you never want to forget.
13. "A penny saved is a penny earned." Would you rather save money or spend it? Why?
14. A genie has just told you that you can trade places with anyone in the world for an hour. Who would you absolutely *not* want to trade places with? Why?

1. List ten things your class could do to help the homeless.

2. You don't have any money but would like to give your mother (or father) a special birthday present. What will you do? Write your answer.

3. A new law has been passed to outlaw television. You must live by the law. List ten things you would do instead of watching television.

4. If the teacher left you in charge of the class for an entire week, how would you plan your week? You will be observed and evaluated just as a teacher is. Write your plan.

5. If you were the governor of a state that bordered an ocean, what would you do to protect the ocean from pollution? Write your answer.

6. A new law has been passed that raises the driving age to 35 years old, the age of the safest drivers according to the Insurance Association. Write a persuasive paragraph to convince the lawmakers that someone younger should be allowed to drive.

7. You are attending the UFO (Unidentified Flying Object) Convention. You are the keynote speaker and must prepare a speech entitled "UFOs—Fact or Fiction." Write this speech.

8. Pretend that you are a parent talking to a child. List ten things that you would want to teach your child.

Patterns

Use with "Critical-Thinking Cards" on page 43.

9. If you were the president of the United States, how would you balance the budget so that the country was not spending more money than it had? Write your suggestions.

10. Think of a way of making electricity that doesn't harm the environment. Explain your idea in a paragraph.

11. Your best friend knocks on your door late one night and is drunk. What do you do? Write your answer.

12. You just had a close encounter with an extraterrestrial. Write a description and draw a picture of this being.

13. You are at a sleepover and someone brings marijuana. Several of your friends start smoking it. What do you do? Write your answer.

14. You are a television programmer. Plan your perfect night of television.

15. You are a world-famous archaeologist who has just discovered the most unusual prehistoric bones ever unearthed. It is your job to piece together the story behind these bones. Describe what this animal looked like and what its life was like. Draw a picture of this life-form and its environment.

16. Your school is preparing a time capsule to put away until the year 2100. List ten things you would put into the time capsule to tell the people of the future what life is like today.

17. Name ten things your family could do to clean up the environment.

18. The five-year-old you are baby-sitting is being totally obnoxious. In a paragraph, describe how you would handle this child.

19. You want a computer more than anything else in the world, but your family cannot afford one. What can you do to get a computer? Devise a plan to achieve your goal.

20. You are an architect who has been asked to design a school. Draw a design of the perfect school. Label each area.

21. You are an architect who has been asked to design a playground. Draw the perfect playground. Label each area.

22. A major food company has asked you for advice. They want you to create the perfect snack food for kids! It must be nutritious, delicious, safe for your teeth and heart, and a hit with kids! Describe and name this snack.

23. Congress just passed a law similar to a Japanese law that requires all children to go to school on Saturday morning. Write five advantages and five disadvantages of this law.

24. The English language grows each year as new words are created. Be a "wordologist" and create five new words. Include the "official" spelling, pronunciation, and meaning of each of these new words. Write each word in a sentence to show how it would be used.

Patterns

Use with "Critical-Thinking Cards" on page 43.

25. A friend just gave you a birthday present—a book you've already read. In a paragraph, describe how you'll handle this situation.

26. If the principal wanted to know what changes you thought were needed to make the school better, what five things would you suggest?

27. Look into the future. It's 30 years from now. Describe what life is like.

28. You have been asked to be chairperson of Earth Day, a day to think about the preservation of the earth. What programs would you work on to protect the environment? Describe them in a paragraph.

29. You have been asked by a world-famous director to star in a movie. Name this movie and your character. Describe the film.

30. S.O.A.S., the Stamp Out Appliances Society, has come to you and said that you and your family may have only one appliance in your house. What appliance will you keep and why?

31. Velcro® is a nylon fabric fastener that binds things together without a button, zipper, buckle, or glue. The people who make this product want to advertise the many uses of Velcro®. Think of ten unique uses for Velcro®. Make a poster advertising these functions.

32. Describe the transportation of the future. List ten of its features. Draw a picture of this vehicle.

CHILLY CHOICES

Pattern

Use with "Alphabet Soup" on page 47.

Illinois Lloyd (cousin of the famous Indiana Jones) craves adventures—but he craves alphabet soup even more! Choose one of the following activities from Lloyd's soup pot.

- Make a list of verbs using the letters in *alphabet*.

- Write a sentence that uses each letter of the alphabet at least once.

- List the alphabet down the side of your paper. Using an encyclopedia to help you, write the Morse code symbol for each letter.

- Here's a real challenge! Write a paragraph in which all of the words are in alphabetical order. The first word must begin with an *a*, the second word with a *b*, and so on.

- List as many words as you can which, when reversed, spell new words (such as *saw* and *was).*

- What is valuable to you? List the alphabet down the side of your paper. For each letter, write something that you think is valuable.

- Write an adjective and a noun for every letter of the alphabet (for example, an *attractive* aardvark, a *boisterous ballplayer,* etc.).

- List as many state abbreviations as you can (for example, *UT* for Utah). Write the name of the state beside its abbreviation. Ask a friend to check your spelling.

- Choose one letter of the alphabet. Write an original tongue twister using the letter. Remember: each word in the tongue twister must begin with your chosen letter.

- List the alphabet down the side of your paper. Try writing an abbreviation for each letter of the alphabet. Include the meaning of the abbreviation (for example *Apr.—April).*

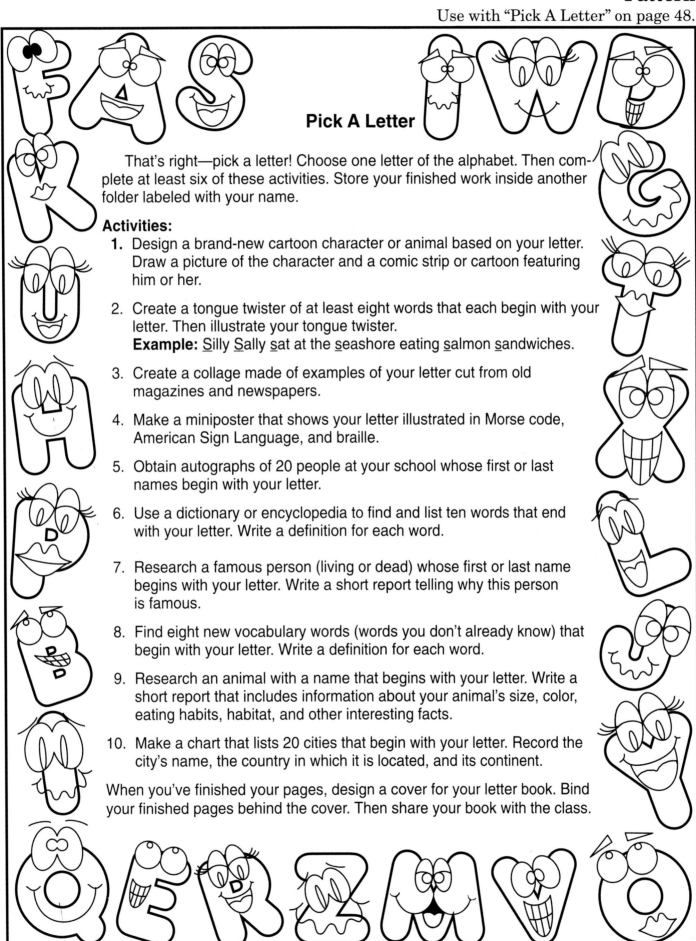

Pick A Letter

That's right—pick a letter! Choose one letter of the alphabet. Then complete at least six of these activities. Store your finished work inside another folder labeled with your name.

Activities:

1. Design a brand-new cartoon character or animal based on your letter. Draw a picture of the character and a comic strip or cartoon featuring him or her.

2. Create a tongue twister of at least eight words that each begin with your letter. Then illustrate your tongue twister.
   Example: <u>S</u>illy <u>S</u>ally <u>s</u>at at the <u>s</u>eashore eating <u>s</u>almon <u>s</u>andwiches.

3. Create a collage made of examples of your letter cut from old magazines and newspapers.

4. Make a miniposter that shows your letter illustrated in Morse code, American Sign Language, and braille.

5. Obtain autographs of 20 people at your school whose first or last names begin with your letter.

6. Use a dictionary or encyclopedia to find and list ten words that end with your letter. Write a definition for each word.

7. Research a famous person (living or dead) whose first or last name begins with your letter. Write a short report telling why this person is famous.

8. Find eight new vocabulary words (words you don't already know) that begin with your letter. Write a definition for each word.

9. Research an animal with a name that begins with your letter. Write a short report that includes information about your animal's size, color, eating habits, habitat, and other interesting facts.

10. Make a chart that lists 20 cities that begin with your letter. Record the city's name, the country in which it is located, and its continent.

When you've finished your pages, design a cover for your letter book. Bind your finished pages behind the cover. Then share your book with the class.

Pattern

Use with "Spooky Sweet Tooth" on page 50.

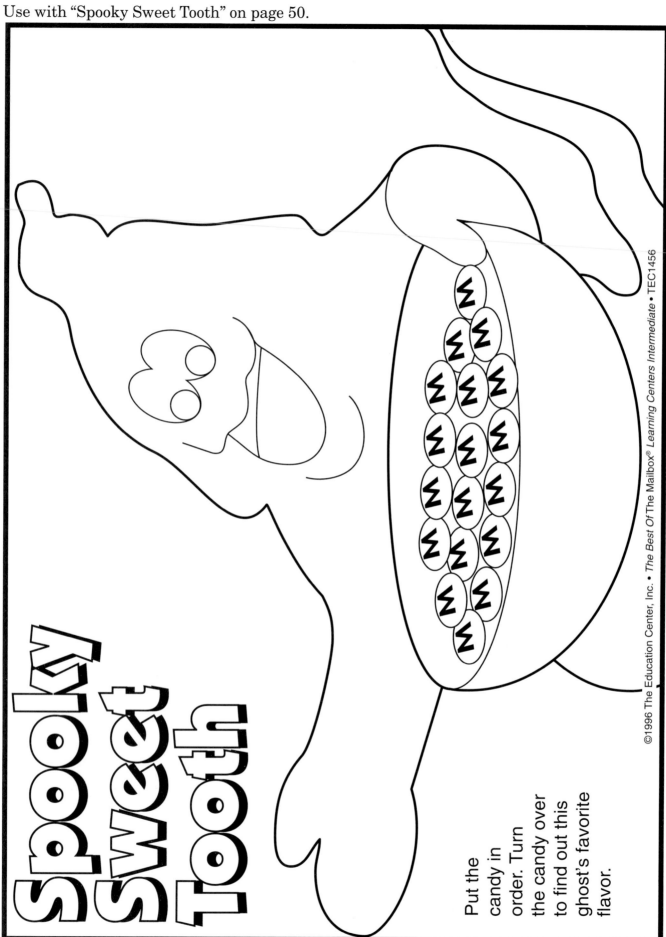

Spooky Sweet Tooth

Put the
candy in
order. Turn
the candy over
to find out this
ghost's favorite
flavor.

Mr. Jones' Bones

Bone up on your math! Write the answer to each problem in its matching bone.

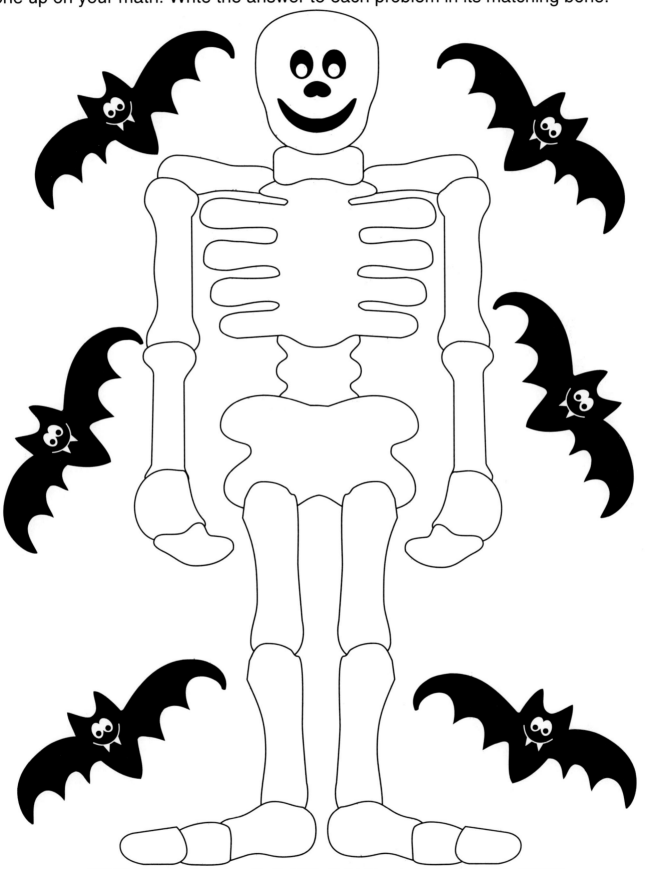

The Most Ghosts

1.
2.
3.

Solve each problem on your paper. Use the key to check. Which room has the most ghosts?

4.
5.
6.

7.
8.
9.

10.
11.
12.

13.
14.
15.

1. Write ten reasons why December should be increased to include 40 days instead of 31.

2. Write a national anthem for the North Pole. Use the tune from a familiar song, or create an original tune.

3. Write an ad for the Yellow Pages describing a store that sells toys which are guaranteed not to break.

4. Design and write a greeting card to give to someone the day after Christmas Day.

5. Design an advertising poster for a new movie, *Revenge Of The Shopping Mall Santas.*

6. Write three alliterative sentences about the holiday season.
   Example: Caroline collected colorful candy canes and coconut Christmas cookies in her corner cupboard.

7. Your feet do a lot of walking while you shop for holiday presents. Write an ode to your fabulous feet. (An *ode* is a type of poem that doesn't have to rhyme.)

8. Describe your newest invention—a machine that is guaranteed to keep little brothers and sisters from messing with your holiday presents. Draw a picture of the invention.

Patterns

Use with "December Writing Cards" on page 52.

9. Write the life story of a snowman.

10. Finish this sentence: I think I'll skip December this year because…

I think I will skip December this year because it's too cold.

11. Write *A Guide To Buying A Gift For An Aunt That You Barely Know.* Include pictures.

How To Buy That Special Gift

12. Design a label for a can of "Instant Holiday Spirit." Don't forget to include the ingredients, too!

INSTANT HOLIDAY SPIRIT

13. You've just kidnapped Santa Claus. Write a ransom note to the police explaining your demands.

I have kid/nap PED SantA…

14. Write a creative fib explaining why all of the presents that your parents hid from you are now lying opened inside the hall closet.

15. A *couplet* is two lines of poetry that rhyme. Write two couplets about holidays other than Christmas.
Example:
On Halloween night, will the moon be aglow? Will witches fly by and cackle, "HELLO"?

16. An *anecdote* is a short story about something that has happened in your life. Write an anecdote about your most unforgettable holiday.

It was the Christmas before my sixth birthday, and Santa brought me a puppy. I was so surprised! I had ALWAYS wanted a puppy. I named her Lady. She was black with white

17. List all of the words that you can think of to describe a snowy day. Now write a description of a snowy day <u>without</u> using any of the words on your list.

18. Describe a holiday gift you really hope you *won't* get this year. Explain why you don't want it.

19. Describe the perfect holiday gift for:
— a forgetful elf who was just fired by Santa
— Bigfoot
— the richest person in the world
— the Chicago Bears football team
Choose one.

20. Write a poem in the shape of a candy cane or holiday wreath.

Christmas joys, more than toys. Time to share, friends who care.

21. Describe a toy that you've invented using only things from your kitchen. Draw a picture of the toy.

22. Write a conversation between a Christmas stocking and a broken candy cane which has been placed inside it.

23. Write several warnings to people who wait until December 24 to do their holiday shopping.

Reminder: Just **15 days** till Christmas!

24. Make a time line showing the major events that have happened to you since last December.

Patterns

Use with "December Writing Cards" on page 52.

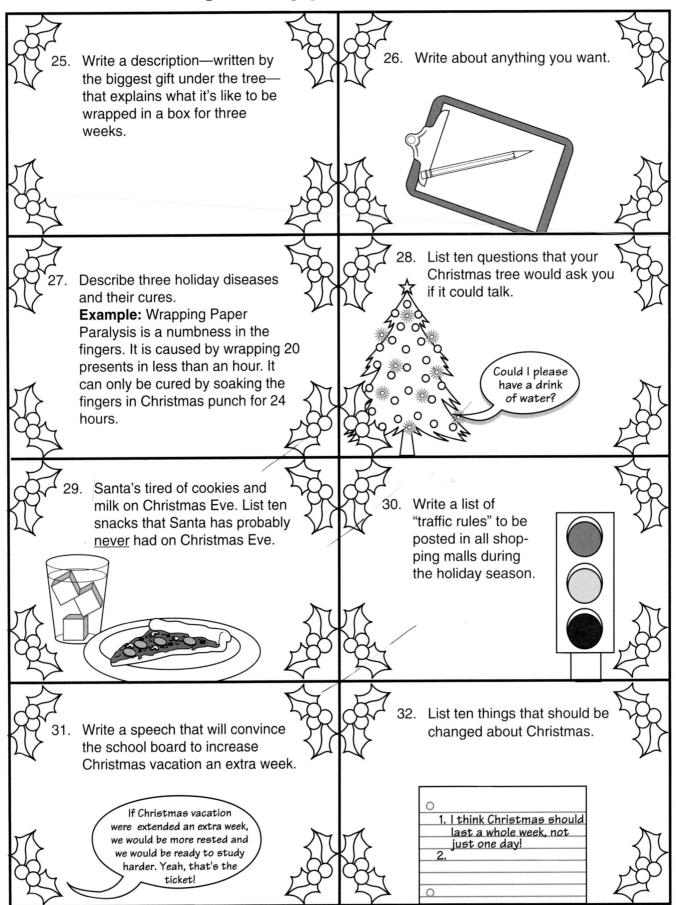

25. Write a description—written by the biggest gift under the tree—that explains what it's like to be wrapped in a box for three weeks.

26. Write about anything you want.

27. Describe three holiday diseases and their cures.
Example: Wrapping Paper Paralysis is a numbness in the fingers. It is caused by wrapping 20 presents in less than an hour. It can only be cured by soaking the fingers in Christmas punch for 24 hours.

28. List ten questions that your Christmas tree would ask you if it could talk.

Could I please have a drink of water?

29. Santa's tired of cookies and milk on Christmas Eve. List ten snacks that Santa has probably <u>never</u> had on Christmas Eve.

30. Write a list of "traffic rules" to be posted in all shopping malls during the holiday season.

31. Write a speech that will convince the school board to increase Christmas vacation an extra week.

If Christmas vacation were extended an extra week, we would be more rested and we would be ready to study harder. Yeah, that's the ticket!

32. List ten things that should be changed about Christmas.

1. I think Christmas should last a whole week, not just one day!
2.

Patterns

Use with "Afro-American History Month Activity Cards" on page 53.

1.

George Washington Carver (1864–1943) was a great scientist. He believed that he could help the poor in the South by teaching them about farming. He made more than 300 products from the peanut plant, including face powder, ink, and soap. He also worked to improve understanding between blacks and whites.

To Do: In 1939, Carver received a medal for his contributions to science. Design a medal to give to George Washington Carver.

2.

Bill Cosby (1937–) is a comedian and was the star of his own program, "The Cosby Show." He costarred in the mid-'60s in the action series "I Spy." He also created and hosted the "Fat Albert and the Cosby Kids" cartoon. Cosby has sold more comedy records than anyone in the world. He's also the author of several popular books.

To Do: Bill Cosby played the father of five children on "The Cosby Show." He also has five children of his own. List at least five things you think fathers should know about raising kids.

3.

Jackie Robinson (1919–1972) was the first black player to play American major league baseball. He played for the Brooklyn Dodgers in 1947. His first year was a hard one. Many people believed a black man didn't belong in the major leagues. But Jackie didn't give up. He helped the Dodgers win six National League pennants and the 1955 World Series.

To Do: Jackie Robinson helped to make it possible for other black players to play in the major leagues. Design a certificate honoring Jackie for his contributions to sports and civil rights.

4.

Sojourner Truth (1797?–1883) was the first black woman to make speeches against slavery. She worked to improve life for blacks living in Washington, DC. She also helped to find jobs and homes in the city for escaped slaves.

To Do: You are preparing to make a speech about a problem that is very important to you. Someone has warned you that there may be some people in the audience who disagree with you. Will you still make your speech? Why or why not? Write your answer.

Patterns

Use with "Afro-American History Month Activity Cards" on page 53.

6.

Mary McLeod Bethune (1875–1955) worked to improve educational opportunities for blacks. Because there were no schools for black children in her hometown, Mary didn't start school until she was 11 years old. After college, she became a teacher. She opened a school for black girls in Florida. This school became Bethune-Cookman College. Mary later worked in the United States government to help end racial discrimination.

To Do: Mary McLeod Bethune believed that education would help black people fight discrimination. How do you think your education will help you 20 years from now? Write your answer in paragraph form.

5.

Langston Hughes (1902–1967) was a writer and poet. He wrote about the inequality suffered by blacks in America. He also wrote plays and humorous stories about black life. These stories were known as the Simple stories because the main character was a wise man nicknamed "Simple."

To Do: Langston Hughes wrote many poems about the lives and problems of black people. Write a poem about your own life and some of the problems you face.

8.

Shirley Chisholm (1924–) is the first black woman to serve in the United States Congress. Chisholm was a member of the House of Representatives from 1969–1983. She worked hard to serve the people that she represented in New York. She also worked to make sure our country's laws met the needs of more people.

To Do: Shirley Chisholm's parents advised her: "Keep your head high. Always give the best you have within you to give. Somebody will recognize it in the future." Do you agree or disagree? Write your answer.

7.

Frederick Douglass (1818–1895) lived a hard life as a slave in the South. Eventually he escaped to the North and freedom. At the age of 24 he made his first speech against slavery. He also founded a newspaper. He was devoted to ending slavery and fighting for black rights. Douglass also helped recruit blacks for the Union Army during the Civil War.

To Do: Frederick Douglass fought hard to end slavery in America. What injustice or problem would you like to see come to an end? Divide a piece of paper in half. On one half, illustrate the problem. On the other half, illustrate a possible solution.

Patterns

Use with "Afro-American History Month Activity Cards" on page 53.

10.

Thurgood Marshall (1908–1993) became the first black ever appointed to serve on the United States Supreme Court. He started his career as a lawyer. Marshall worked to eliminate separate schools for blacks and whites.

To Do: Thurgood Marshall believed in protecting human rights. Write a letter to Justice Marshall. Tell him what you think are the rights of school children.

12.

Coretta Scott King (1927–) works for the civil rights of blacks and other minorities. She is the widow of Dr. Martin Luther King, Jr. While her husband was working to win more rights for black Americans, Mrs. King gave speeches and lectures. After Dr. King was killed, Mrs. King continued working for civil rights.

To Do: What rights do you think all Americans should enjoy? Make a list of at least ten of these rights.

9.

Matthew Henson (1866–1955) worked as the captain's cabin boy on a boat. He loved traveling. Later Matthew worked for Robert Peary, a naval engineer. When Peary decided to try to reach the North Pole, Matthew was hired to go with him. After several failures, they reached the North Pole. Matthew was chosen to plant the American flag in the frozen ground.

To Do: Matthew Henson was the first man to set foot on the North Pole. What would you like to be the first person to do? Write your answer.

11.

Charles Richard Drew (1904–1950) almost became a professional football player. But instead he decided to become a doctor. He is known for setting up some of the nation's first blood banks. His blood banks saved many lives, particularly during World War II.

To Do: Charles Drew once resigned from a job. The reason? He was told to collect and store blood donated by black people separately from blood donated by whites. Write a letter to Charles Drew telling him what you think of his decision to resign.

Patterns

Use with "Afro-American History Month Activity Cards" on page 53.

13.

Althea Gibson (1927–) became one of the world's greatest tennis players. She was the first black to play at Wimbledon, England. She won many tennis titles. After she retired from tennis, she became a professional golfer.

To Do: Do some research about another famous black female athlete, Wilma Rudolph. How are she and Althea Gibson alike? How are they different? Write your answer.

14.

Jesse Jackson (1941–) is an American civil rights activist, political leader, and Baptist minister. In 1984 and 1988 he ran for the Democratic nomination for president. Even though he did not win either time, he focused attention on the problems of blacks and other minority groups in America. His work includes helping black students get a better education.

To Do: Pretend that Jesse Jackson has asked you to write a plan. The plan should convince kids like yourself to stay away from drugs and alcohol. Write your plan. Tell why you think it could work.

15.

Garrett Morgan (1877–1963) invented the first gas mask. It was called the Morgan Safety Hood. It saved many lives. He and his brother once used the masks to rescue 32 men from a tunnel explosion. Garrett also invented the first traffic-light signal.

To Do: Think of a problem (big or small) in the world today. Now think of an invention that might solve that problem. Draw a picture of your invention. Give it a name. Write a brief description of how your invention works.

16.

Paul Robeson (1898–1976) was an outstanding actor and singer. He was featured in many movies and on many record albums. Robeson performed in many famous plays. He also worked in the peace and civil rights movements of the late 1930s.

To Do: Paul Robeson was a man of many talents. He was a star athlete in college, a singer and actor, a civil rights activist, and even an author. Everyone has talents. Make a collage to illustrate some of your talents.